The Forgotten Desi and Lucy TV Projects:
The Desilu Series and Specials that Might Have Been

By Richard Irvin

The Forgotten Desi and Lucy TV Projects: The Desilu Series and Specials that Might Have Been
By Richard Irvin
Copyright © 2020 Richard Irvin
No part of this book may be reproduced in any form or by any means, electronic, mechanical, digital, photocopying, or recording, except for inclusion of a review, without permission in writing from the publisher or Author.

Published in the USA by:
BearManor Media
4700 Millenia Blvd.
Suite 175 PMB 90497
Orlando, FL 32839
www.bearmanormedia.com

Paperback ISBN: 978-1-62933-545-2
Case ISBN: 978-1-62933-546-9
BearManor Media, Orlando, Florida
Printed in the United States of America
Book design by Robbie Adkins, www.adkinsconsult.com

Table of Contents

Acknowledgements ix
Preface xi
Chapter 1: Desilu's Funny Lady Comedy Series 1
   I Love Lucy 1
   Willy 4
   December Bride 6
   Those Whiting Girls 7
   The Ann Sothern Show 8
   The Lucy Show 9
Chapter 2: Desi's Unsold Funny Lady Pilots 11
   Just Off Broadway 11
   Adventures of a Model 12
   Ernestine 13
   All about Barbara 14
   Gussie, My Girl 15
   Always April 16
   Pandora 17
   Oh, Nurse 18
Chapter 3: Desi's Unsold Funny Guys Pilots 19
   Eddie Quillan Project 19
   Ritz Brothers 19
   The Bob Hope Show 20
   Sad Sack 20
   Night Watchman 20
   Where There's Smokey 20
   Aldo Ray Project 21
   My Wife's Brother 21
   College Humor 22
   Swingin' Together 22
Chapter 4: Desi's Unsold Funny Couples Pilots 24
   The Rolling Stones 24
   You're Only Young Twice 24
   The Mertzes 25

Guestward Ho! 27
Three in a Row 28
Cloud Nine 28
Man of Letters 28
Phil Harris/Alice Faye Show 29
You Can't Win Them All 30
The Holidays Abroad 31
Mickey and the Contessa 32
The Two of Us 32
Spanner 33
Chapter 5: Desi's Purely Fictional Unsold Drama Attempts 34
Downbeat 34
Fast Freight 35
Country Doctor 35
Mr. Tutt 36
The Black Arrow 37
The Wildcatters 37
Rookie Cop 37
The Last Marshal 38
Personal Report, Inc. 38
Tonight in Havana 39
Abbott Mysteries 39
Private Eyeful 39
Security Agent 40
Chick Bowdrie, Texas Ranger 41
Caballero 41
Homicide Squad (aka *Homicide*) 42
Young Man with a Badge 42
Sheriff Squad 42
The Violators 44
Adventures of Jack London 44
The Guardians 44
The Big Circuit 44
Locust 4-3931 45
Chapter 6: Desi's Somewhat Reality-Based Unsold Drama Pilots ... 46
Tales of Allan Pinkerton (aka *The Pinkerton Story*) 47
Father Duffy of Hell's Kitchen 47

Cowboy Detective 49
The Flying Fish 49
John Wesley Hardin Family Project 49
Privateer 50
Intelligence Squad 50
Dallas 51
Secret Service Agent 52
Ten Top Wanted Men 52
The Man from Telegraph Hill 53
O.C.D. (Official Crime Division) 54
No Man Walks Alone 54
Chapter 7: Desilu's Unsold Anthology Pilots 55
   Anthology of Suspense 55
   The Orson Welles Show 56
   Woman in the Case 59
   Famous Artists Anthologies 61
   The Arlene Dahl Show 62
   For Men Only 63
   Villa Marina 63
   Anatomy of... 64
   Victor Borge Comedy Theatre 64
   The United States Immigration Story 65
Chapter 8: *Westinghouse-Desilu Playhouse* Spin-offs 67
   U.S. Air Force 74
   Bandwagon 76
   Nightclub 77
   Donegan's Six Guns 78
   Johnny Cinderella 78
Chapter 9: Unsold *Kraft Mystery Theatre* Spin-offs 80
   Dr. Augustus Van Dusen Mysteries 80
   Duncan Maclain Mysteries 83
Chapter 10: *The Untouchables* Inspired Unsold Pilots 84
   C.I.C. (Counter-Intelligence Corps) 84
   The White Knights 87
   The Seekers 89
   Floyd Gibbons: Reporter 90
   The Con Man 91

Chapter 11: Desilu's Unsold Kid and Game Show Pilots 93
   Jon Whiteley/Vincent Winter Project 93
   Rikki of the Islands (aka Jungle Boy) 94
   By the Numbers.. 95
   Zoom.. 95
   Relatively Yours 95
Chapter 12: Desilu's Unproduced Lucy Movies and TV Specials.... 97
   Desi and Lucy's Movie Plans 97
     Blazing Beulah from Butte................................ 97
     Venus Mahoney... 98
     The Star.. 98
     That Townsend Girl 99
   Lucy's Solo Possibilities 99
     By the Beautiful Sea 100
     By Jupiter!.. 101
     Serial Queen 102
     Next Week, East Lynne................................. 102
     Size 12.. 104
     Texas Guinan Project 106
     Fancy Meeting You Again 106
     Happy Birthday.. 107
     "The Widow with the Serpent's Tongue" 109
     Fanny 110
     Sweet Jab in the Morning................................ 111
   The "Almost" *I Love Lucy* Cast Reunion: *"Lucy Goes to Broadway"* ..112
   Lucy in Europe and Elsewhere. 116
Chapter 13: Other Desilu Unproduced Specials 117
   Don Quixote... 117
   The Industrialists 117
Chapter 14: Lucy's Unsold Funny Lady Comedy Pilots 119
   Maggie Brown 121
   Working Girls.. 123
   A-Okay O'Shea... 123
   Exclusively Connie.. 124
   The Lady Is a Champ 124
   Mother Is the Law (aka Mrs. Keystone and the Kops).............. 126
   The Pearls 127

My Lucky Penny 127
Chapter 15: Lucy's Unsold Funny Men Comedy Pilots 129
   Hey, Teacher 129
   The Hoofer 129
   Papa G.I. 131
   My Uncle Louie 131
   The Farmer from Palermo 132
   My Son, The Doctor 133
   The Recruiters 134
   His Highness and O'Hara 134
Chapter 16: Lucy's Unsold Parody and Fantasy Comedy Pilots 135
   The Unteachables 135
   I Married a Martian 136
   Hooray for Hollywood 137
   Vacation with Pay 137
   The Good Old Days 138
   Corky/ Love Me, Love Queenie 139
   Frank Merriwell 139
   EM + C2, Inc. 140
   Penelope's Boys 141
   Alfred of the Amazon 141
Chapter 17: Lucy's Unsold Drama Pilots 143
   Spellbound 143
   The Greenhorns 143
   Borderline 144
   Cleat Adams 144
   Escapade 144
   The Long Hunt of April Savage 144
   The Night Hunters 146
Chapter 18: Gene Roddenberry's Unsold and Rejected Desilu Pilots . 147
   High Noon 147
   The Whirlwind 148
   Code 100 148
   Blood, Of the A.E.F. 149
   Police Story 149
   Star Trek – "The Cage" 150
   Assignment: Earth 153

Yankee Gunfighter.. 154
Chapter 19: Precursors to *Mission: Impossible* 155
   The Man Nobody Knows 156
   Trio... 156
Chapter 20: Desi Arnaz Productions............................ 158
   The Carol Channing Show.................................... 160
   Gussie, My Girl (second attempt) 161
   Ham and Davey.. 162
   Land's End... 163
   Chairman of the Board...................................... 163
   Dr. Domingo 164
Chapter 21: Lucille Ball Productions.......................... 166
   "Diamond Jim and Lillian Russell"............................ 166
   The Lucie Arnaz Show (aka *Kim*) 170
   The Music Mart 171
   Bungle Abbey 172
Appendix A: The Comedy Episodes that Might Have Been 176
   I Love Lucy.. 176
   Willy 177
   The Ann Sothern Show....................................... 178
   The Lucy Show 179
Endnotes 184
Index 187

Acknowledgements

The author would like to thank the following institutions and individuals for their help with this book:

UCLA Library Special Collections for information from the Norman Lessing papers 1943-1982, Albert Zugsmith papers 1950-1968, Edward Jurist papers 1940-1979, Martin Berkeley Collection of Television and Motion Picture Scripts, 1940-ca.-1960, Hal Goodman papers 1940-1993, Ann Sothern Collection, Janice Schwarz Collection, Jimmy Durante Collection, Collections of Television Series Scripts, and RKO Radio Pictures records, circa 1921-circa 1956;

UCLA Film and Television Archives for making available viewing copies of various Desilu pilots;

The Margaret Harrick Library for material from the Bert Granet Papers and the Lloyd Bacon Papers;

The Writer's Guild Foundation for a copy of a Desilu pilot treatment by Adrian Spies;

California State University LA JFK Memorial Library staff for summarizing the story line of the *Father Duffy of Hell's Kitchen* script;

Popular Culture Library, Bowling Green State University for copies of scripts from its *Desilu Playhouse* collection;

Wisconsin Center of Film and Theatre Research for information from the Bruce Geller Papers, David Harmon Papers, Richard Nash Collection, William Spier and June Havoc Collection, Adrian Spies Collection, and Norman Katkov Papers;

San Diego State University for copies of treatments and scripts from the Desi Arnaz Collection;

American Heritage Center at the University of Wyoming for copies of scripts from the Jack Donohue Collection, the Sam Rolfe Collection and the Isobel Lennart Collection;

Thousand Oaks Library Foundation for a copy of a script from its Special Collections;

University of Iowa for information from the Robert Blees Papers and the Arthur Ross Papers;

University of Oregon for material from the Charles Marquis Warren Papers;

University of Illinois for a copy of a script from its TV Script Collection;

Yale University for information from the Max Wilk Collection;

Indiana University for information from the McGreevy Papers;

University of Texas at Austin Library for material from the James Pinckney Papers, 1939-1999;

Edward Comstock from the Cinematic Arts Library at the University of Southern California for his great help in providing files on Desilu pilots as well as material from the Dan Duryea Collection;

Library of Congress, Motion Picture and TV Reading Room staff for making available viewing copies of many Desilu pilots and the Manuscript Division for information from the Lucy Kroll Papers; and

Garry Settimi for proofing and editing the manuscript.

Preface

While many books have been written about Lucille Ball and Desi Arnaz, particularly the former, as well as the iconic television series produced by their company, Desilu, such as *I Love Lucy*, *The Lucy Show*, *The Untouchables*, *Mission: Impossible*, and *Star Trek*, this is the only work that describes in detail the unsold television pilots and unproduced specials contemplated by Desilu. The Desilu television series that might have been range from ones starring Bob Hope, Arlene Dahl, and Frank Sinatra to several spin-offs and take-offs on *The Untouchables*. The unproduced specials include ones that would have starred Lucille Ball as Fanny Brice in a pre-*Funny Girl* presentation, a special "Lucy Goes to Broadway" that would have reunited most of the cast from *I Love Lucy*, and one that would have featured Jackie Gleason and Lucy as Diamond Jim Brady and Lillian Russell. These and many more television projects are chronicled in this book.

Archives from the University of Southern California describing television pilots considered by production companies in the 1950s and 1960s were the main source for identifying the unsold Desilu pilots detailed in this work. An internal memo found among Desilu producer Bert Granet's papers at the Margaret Herrick Library formed the basis of the chapter about most of the unproduced Lucille Ball specials.

In spring 1950, Lucille Ball and Desi Arnaz formed their own production company. Desi became president of the company with Lucy as vice president. As columnist Gene Handsaker described, "During business discussions, Desi may wear a hat labeled 'Pres,' while Lucy wears one lettered 'Veepee'... During rehearsals they sometimes switch to headgear reading 'Boy Actor' and 'Girl Actor.'"[1]

Before being sold to Gulf and Western Industries and merged with Paramount in 1967, Desilu had only two presidents - Desi Arnaz from

1950 until his resignation in November 1962 and Lucille Ball from 1962 to 1967. Each had their own management style.

Variety described Arnaz's management of the company thusly, "Desilu has typified the one-man operation, but its position has tended to fluctuate with the erratic working habits of the man, Desi Arnaz... all the creative decisions have been made by Arnaz who has tended to operate in cycles, with occasional bursts of creative effort spaced by extensive layoffs away from the studio."[2]

Desi hired Martin Leeds from CBS, who joined Desilu in 1953 as executive vice president in charge of production and ran the business and sales operations of the company until he left in 1960 after a falling out with Arnaz.

Under Desi's presidency, the company launched the hit series *I Love Lucy*, *December Bride*, *The Lucy Show* and *The Untouchables*, along with several, mostly unmemorable, other series. As for comedy pilots, Desi attempted to recreate the magic of *I Love Lucy* with vehicles for actresses like Joanne Dru, Rose Marie, and Janis Paige. Concerning drama pilots, Mr. Arnaz seemed to prefer ones that fictionalized the lives of real people or the work of government agencies.

Desi Arnaz resigned as Desilu's president in November 1962. There is debate about whether Arnaz was forced out of the company or if he left voluntarily. While Desi's continuing problems with excessive drinking no doubt played a role in his departure, Arnaz, speaking to Hollywood columnist Bob Thomas, indicated that among his reasons for leaving was not being terribly interested in managing a company with 3000 employees. "I enjoyed the creative end – getting together with some writers on an idea, following through with scripts, casting the project and bringing forth the final product" remarked Arnaz. Who went on to say, "But I found myself tied up with a factory operation."[3]

After Desi left, Lucille Ball purchased her ex-husband's interest in Desilu and became the head of the company.

As *The New York Times* reported when Lucy became the president, "Lucille Ball ... said yesterday she had not yet learned much about being president of one of Hollywood's major television production companies. ...'Up until then I had been vice president in charge of dusting... Now I get to sweep up.'"[4]

Lucille Ball's presidency was not without problems. According to Herb Solow, "Lucy was brilliant in knowing what was good for her 'Lucy' character, her writers, her costars, her directors, her show. But she didn't have the foggiest idea how to deal with the networks and the creative community, how to play the television production game."[5] And so, the Ashley-Famous agency and CBS convinced Lucy to hire that network's executive Oscar Katz to make pilots and series. Katz, in turn, hired Herb Solow as the man in charge of the development, sale, and production of pilots and series at the studio.

The new management opened up the studio's development of comedy pilots to a variety of writers that resulted in a wide array of concepts from Dwayne Hickman as an elementary school teacher to his brother Darryl as a caveman to Betty Hutton in a "Lucy-like" family comedy.

Despite being unable to produce a successful comedy series other than her own, under Lucy's presidency the legendary series *Mission: Impossible* and *Star Trek* were launched.

The Forgotten Desi and Lucy TV Projects first describes the comedies and dramas that might have been under Desi's presidency and then the unsold pilots conceived while Lucy was the head of the company. Transitioning between the two presidencies, Chapter 12 details the unproduced TV specials contemplated for Ms. Ball after the end of *I Love Lucy*. The final two chapters of the book look at the series that both Arnaz and Ball attempted to launch when they formed their own separate production companies – Desi Arnaz Productions and Lucille Ball Productions, after Desilu was merged into Paramount. The unsold pilots in each chapter are listed chronologically in order of the dates on which they were first considered.

In addition to producing several pilots and television series, Desilu also rented their facilities and crew out to other companies for filming television shows. For instance, Danny Thomas used Desilu to make series like his own comedy as well as *The Dick Van Dyke Show* and *The Andy Griffith Show*. Series and pilots made by companies other than Desilu but filmed at Desilu Studios are not included in this book.

The author hopes that readers of this book will gain additional insights into the producing careers of both Desi and Lucy and also the kinds of television series contemplated by their production company.

Chapter 1: Desilu's Funny Lady Comedy Series

Under the leadership of Desi Arnaz, Desilu produced several comedies starring mainly females in the 1950s and early 1960s. Before describing the series that might have been, it is important to note the female-centric sitcoms that were.

Lucille Ball and Desi Arnaz, the owners of Desilu Studios and the stars of I Love Lucy.

I Love Lucy

Lucille Ball became a TV comedy legend starring with her husband in Desilu's longest running comedy – *I Love Lucy*, which aired for six seasons from 1951 to 1957 and then for three more seasons in a one-hour format known as the *Lucille Ball-Desi Arnaz Show (aka Lucy-Desi Comedy Hour)* consisting of thirteen special episodes. While Lucille Ball's two subsequent comedies – *The Lucy Show* and *Here's Lucy*, also each ran for six seasons, there were no additional episodes after each series ended. *I Love Lucy* is the only television series from the 1950s that still appears periodically in colorized versions on network TV today.

When Desi and Lucy formed their production company in 1950, *The Los Angeles Times* reported, "They will develop a three-way program including vaudeville units, television shows and motion pictures. First on their program will be the dispatching of a vaudeville company headed by Miss Ball and Arnaz to Chicago Theater June 2, with an engagement to follow at the Roxy Theater, June 9."[6]

The purpose of the vaudeville shows was to determine how the couple would perform together in front of a live audience before launching their own TV series.

In reviewing the Lucille Ball/Desi Arnaz vaudeville act in Chicago, *The Billboard* noted:

> Coupled with her hubby, Desi Arnaz, who's been just average locally in the past, the Hollywood couple stack up as topnotch stage fare. The Carrot-topped comedienne is a real looker with an ingratiating personality. Arnaz confined himself to fine Latin warbling and straighting his frau. Miss Ball is exceptionally versatile, doing songs, trying her hand at the Charleston and contributing a Red Skeltonish bit built around her attempt to get a job with Arnaz's band. The last item fractured 'em. The duo's wind-up, with Arnaz doing his standard Cuban Pete while she comes on as a Brooklyn cutie, won a terrific bow-off mitt.[7]

The comedy routines in the vaudeville act were written by Bob Carroll, Jr. and Madelyn Pugh, two writers from Lucy's radio comedy at the time called *My Favorite Husband*. Lucy played Liz Cugat on the show, the wife of George Cugat (Richard Denning). Premiering on July 23, 1948, the Cugat's were an upper-middle class couple with George working at a bank and Liz involved in society matters. Carroll Jr., Pugh, and producer/writer Jess Oppenheimer took over writing the series in fall 1948, changed the last name of the characters to "Cooper," and made the couple more middle-class. The couple often interacted with George's boss, Rudolph (Gale Gordon) and his wife, Iris (Bea Benaderet).

In 1950, when the sponsor of the radio series decided to bring *My Favorite Husband* to television, it wanted Richard Denning to continue to portray George. However, Lucy insisted that her real-life husband play her partner. To prove that audiences would accept the pair as husband and wife, they did the vaudeville shows. Hence, the birth of *I Love Lucy* with Desi Arnaz playing Ricky Ricardo and Lucille appearing as Lucy Ricardo. Instead of Gale Gordon and Bea Benaderet continuing their roles from *My Favorite Husband*, William Frawley and Vivian Vance were hired to play Fred and Ethel Mertz, the couple's landlords and best friends.

Writers Carroll Jr, Pugh, and Oppenheimer continued with *I Love Lucy* adapting many of the scripts from *My Favorite Husband* for the television comedy.

A December 25, 1948 installment of *My Favorite Husband*, "Numerology" had Liz becoming involved with numerology, horoscopes, and Ouija boards. Upon learning that the Cooper's landlord, Mr. Curry, is also into numerology and who, based on the "advice" from his late wife, Bernice, wants to raise the Cooper's rent, Liz decides to hold a séance and invite Curry. Liz has their neighbor, Mr. Wood, who plays a fortune teller at the local fair, conduct the séance. Liz, standing behind a curtain, pretends she is the voice of Bernice Curry telling her husband from beyond the grave not to raise the Cooper's rent. However, the plan backfires when Curry, angry at all the years of being henpecked by Bernice, decides to defy her instructions and raises the Cooper's rent even more. After being free for a number of days from Bernice's spirit, Curry has second thoughts and keeps the rent as it is.

If this story sounds familiar, it is. The script was adapted for the November 26, 1951 episode of *I Love Lucy* called "The Séance" with Lucy inviting a theatrical producer, Mr. Merriweather to a séance to convince him to hire Ricky for a new show. In this version, Ethel Mertz played the medium with both Lucy and Fred becoming the voices of Merriweather's cocker spaniel Tillie and his late wife Adelaide. Actor Jay Novello played Mr. Curry on the radio episode and Mr. Merriweather on the TV adaptation. On both versions, George Cooper and Ricky Ricardo were a number five in numerology, Liz/Lucy was a three, and Mr. Curry/Merriweather, a one, prompting the latter to say, "We're all odd, aren't we?"

Several other scripts from *My Favorite Husband* turned into *Lucy* episodes including an April 29, 1949 radio show, "Time Schedule" becoming a May 26, 1952 *I Love Lucy* installment, "Lucy's Schedule;" the radio episode "Liz Develops an Inferiority Complex" adapted as the February 2, 1953 *I Love Lucy* show "Inferiority Complex;" and *My Favorite Husband's* "The Misunderstanding of the Black Eye" transforming into the March 9, 1953 *Lucy* episode, "The Black Eye."

Head writer and producer Jess Oppenheimer left Desilu in 1956. Later during *I Love Lucy's* run, writers Bob Schiller and Bob Weiskopf were brought on board to script episodes along with Madelyn Pugh and Bob Carroll, Jr. The four writers as well as Oppenheimer would have an off-again, on-again relationship with Desilu throughout their careers as indicated in subsequent chapters.

I Love Lucy was known not only for talent of Lucille Ball performing physical comedy stunts, which played very well on the visual medium of television, but also for the use of big-name guest stars in later episodes. The success of *Lucy* and the support of CBS led to Desilu expanding production to make other shows and pilots. In 1954, the company sold two comedy series to CBS – both featuring single female central characters.

Willy

Together with Louis Pelletier, William Spier, who had a lengthy career as a Desilu writer and producer, created the comedy, *Willy*, for Mrs. Spier – June Havoc. The Desilu show went through various title changes (i.e., *The Artful Miss Dodger* and *My Aunt Willy*) before being called simply *Willy*. The series sponsor, General Mills, initially scheduled the series on ABC but made a last minute change and moved it to CBS.

Willa Dodger has just received her law degree from night school and opens a practice in her New Hampshire hometown. She lives with her father Walter (Lloyd Corrigan), her sister Emily (Mary Treen), and her nephew, Franklin (Danny Richards, Jr.). Although a career woman, Willa had a love interest on the show, Charlie Bush (Whitefield Connor), who was pressuring her to give up law and settle down with him.

Scheduled for 10:30 on Saturday nights, Desi Arnaz appeared at the beginning of the first show on September 18, 1954 to introduce the series and give a plug for General Mills. The pilot had Willy taking on the case of Franklin's friend from school whose dog may be put to sleep because he chased a farmer's cow. The cow will now not produce milk. Willy shows that the dog was not chasing the cow but herding the animal back to its own property after it had strayed. The local paper reports, "Willa Dodger refuses to be cowed! Dog families victorious in hoofy tussle." Turns out that the cow wasn't producing milk because it was pregnant.

At midseason, the format of the show changed with Willa moving to New York City to work as legal counsel for American Variety Artists. The change in setting was to broaden the comedy and take advantage of Ms. Havoc's dancing talent. As a newspaper article about the change of setting pointed out at the time, "June . . . can be less restrained as attorney for a show business organization than as a small town lady lawyer."[8]

In the debut of the new setting, Willy starts working for Perry Bannister, her boss at American Variety Artists. However, Bannister is disappointed that his new hire is a female thinking he was hiring "William Dodger." He doesn't give her any assignments simply waiting for her four-week contract to end. She points out to him that her contract can't be terminated unless he gives her at least one project. Bannister assigns Willy to attend opening night at a club to make sure that the chorus line includes six girls. One of the girls is Sheila Bannister, Perry's daughter. Miffed when she isn't given the principal spot in the line when a dancer falls ill, Sheila leaves, and so Willy takes her spot. Bannister, in the audience, fires Willy for taking over his daughter's role as a dancer. Sheila later visits Willy to apologize for her unprofessional behavior at the nightclub. Bannister stops by Willy's apartment and overhears his daughter telling Willy that Ms. Dodger showed what it really means to be a professional in show business. Bannister asks Willy to stay on as the attorney for the organization.

Introducing a show business theme into *Willy* was one of the hallmarks of many Desilu comedies originating of course with *I Love Lucy* with Lucy Ricardo's attempts to enter the business and Ricky's occupation as a full-time entertainer.

Willy was later moved to 10:30 Thursday nights. But the format and time slot changes didn't pull in a bigger audience, and the show was gone at the end of the 1954-55 season. In 1960, Arnaz and Ms. Havoc discussed another series possibility on which she might star but nothing came of those discussions.

December Bride

While its time slot worked to the disadvantage of *Willy*, Desi's other sitcom launched in 1954 greatly benefited from being scheduled on Monday's at 9:30 following *I Love Lucy*. *December Bride* starring Spring Byington was an adaptation of the radio series of the same name and became a top ten ratings hit until in its final fifth season when the show was moved to Thursdays at 8:00 pm. Byington appeared as Lily Ruskin, a sprightly widow who moves in with her daughter, Ruth and son-in-law, Matt Henshaw.

Parke Levy, who created *December Bride*, approached Desi Arnaz about making the TV pilot. CBS had dropped its option on turning the radio series into a television sitcom because the network didn't want Spring Byington as the lead. Arnaz bought fifty percent of the show. After Bill Paley, head of CBS at the time, viewed the pilot, he picked it up as a series. Dismayed that his network executives had dropped the option on the show without his knowledge, Arnaz sold half of his ownership interest (twenty-five percent) back to Paley in return for having the series scheduled right after *I Love Lucy*.

While many of the story lines of *December Bride* concerned Lily's romantic life in attempting to find a suitable mate, several others had Lily and her friend Hilda Crocker (Verna Felton) becoming involved in "Lucy and Ethel" types of situations.

In an October 10, 1955 installment, Hilda and Lily land jobs as waitresses at a run-down pizzeria and organize a "pizzatorium." A March 19, 1956 episode had Lily and Hilda handcuffed together as part of a magic act with predictable complications ensuing when the amateur magician loses the key. Desi Arnaz played himself in a February 1956 show. Arnaz is suing Lily's son-in-law's company for $50,000 because of lack of a retaining wall on a new home next to his which Matt's company is building. Because of no retaining wall, Desi's den dropped four feet. Lily and Hilda decide to visit Desi to talk him out of the suit since Lily feels responsible because she forgot to drop off the blueprints for the project. They masquerade as teenage members of Arnaz's fan club to see him and dance their hearts out with the other teenagers.

Even with *December Bride*, a comedy whose characters had no obvious connection to show business, Desilu still made episodes involving the Lily

Ruskin character involved with entertainment activities. For example, in a January 23, 1956 installment, Lily and Hilda acquire an old Rudy Vallee record. They agree to return it to the crooner if he makes a personal appearance at their women's club. On an April 2, 1959 show, Lily and Hilda try to get a TV role for neighbor Pete Porter's new offspring. Also, as with *I Love Lucy*, later seasons of *December Bride* featured many celebrities playing themselves like Zsa Gabor, Rory Calhoun, Fred MacMurray, and Mickey Rooney.

Those Whiting Girls

One of the funny female comedies launched by Desilu after *I Love Lucy*, *Willy*, and *December Bride* was *Those Whiting Girls* featuring real-life sisters and singers, Margaret and Barbara Whiting. Created by *Lucy* writers, Madelyn Pugh and Bob Carroll, Jr., the series was a summer replacement for *Lucy* in 1955.

Margaret was the "straight woman" of the duo, while the slapstick and hijinks were often left to Barbara a la Lucy Ricardo. Mabel Albertson played the sisters' mother, Eleanor, a combination of Ethel and Fred Mertz, particularly the latter with her acerbic comments. Jerry Paris as Artie appeared as Margaret's piano player. The series continued the show business theme of many Desilu comedies.

A typical episode had Barbara, her mother, and/or Artie often jumping to conclusions about something Margaret is doing. For example, on one show, the family wants to get a glimpse of Margaret's new boyfriend, Dan Simmons, whom Margaret has been keeping away from her sister and mother. When Barbara and Eleanor find out that Margaret has given Dan a check for $1000, they conclude that he is a gigolo. Later, Margaret plans to throw a surprise party for Artie celebrating his seven-year anniversary as her accompanist. After Eleanor learns that a cake will be delivered, she concludes the cake is for Margaret's wedding to Dan. Margaret confronts her family about Dan revealing that the $1000 was a loan to help him finance a classical piano concert for himself and that the cake is a surprise for Artie's party.

On another episode, while taking a psychology course in college, Barbara jumps to the conclusion that her sister evidences "sibling jealousy" meaning that she is envious of the attention paid to her younger sister. Margaret accidentally tears Barbara's favorite blouse and then spills coffee on her sister's sweater leading Barbara to ask her psychology professor to visit her home one evening to observe Margaret. When the professor stops by, he says he is a big fan of Margaret's singing and asks her out to dinner. He tells Barbara that she is the one that has neurotic tendencies.

While never becoming a regular fall through spring series on CBS, *Those Whiting Girls* was picked up again as a summer replacement for *I Love Lucy* in 1957.

The Ann Sothern Show

In 1957, Arnaz negotiated a deal with Ann Sothern for Desilu to co-produce a new situation comedy with Sothern's company, Anso. Originally titled *Career Girl*, the concept had Sothern playing a department store manager. Leonard Gershe wrote the initial pilot scripts. After Sothern disapproved of the Gershe scripts, Desi had Bob Schiller and Bob Weiskopf write a new script with the Sothern character, Katy O'Connor, as an assistant manager of a New York hotel. About the potential series, Desi remarked, "If I don't sell this one, I'll quit the business."[9] On the basis of the pilot, CBS picked up the series for its fall 1958 schedule. The comedy was similar in concept to *Willy* – a single, professional woman dealing with problems that arose out of her work.

Initially, the series co-starred Ernest Truex as the henpecked manager of the hotel; Reta Shaw as his domineering wife; Katy's roommate and secretary played by Ann Tyrrell; Jack Mullaney as the bellhop; and Jacques Scott as the hotel desk clerk. About mid-way through its first season, Don Porter replaced Ernest Truex as the new hotel manager. Porter had played Sothern's boss on her first television series, *Private Secretary*. Ann Tyrell had also been a regular on Sothern's previous comedy.

Typical episodes involved Katy encountering a problem at work and coming up with a comical solution to the issue. On the second episode of the series, "Six Wives Plus Two," a maharajah checks into the Bartley House hotel with six of his eight wives. After Mr. Macauley (Treux) saves the maharajah from being hit by a car, the maharajah gifts one of his wives to the manager. The woman says that she can't be returned to her husband given the customs of her country.

Katy has two problems to solve. First, the new wife must be kept a secret from Mrs. Macauley who is giving a party for all six wives. To resolve this, Katy masquerades as the sixth wife dressed in harem attire to fool Mrs.

Macauley at her party. Second, Katy has to come up with a way to get rid of the new wife. She does this by asking the maharajah to exchange the wife for another gift. Mr. Macauley ends up receiving an elephant as the exchange gift.

In another example, a second season episode had Katy being instructed by her boss, Mr. Devry (Porter), to fire Billy (Joel Grey), a bellhop who had upset Mr. Dooley (Jack Albertson), an important producer staying at the hotel, by trying to audition for him in his hotel room. Katy sees promise in Billy's singing talent. When she learns that Dooley needs to discover talent for himself, she arranges auditions for him in the hotel's Crystal Room where he hears Billy sing. The bellhop receives a part in Dooley's next show.

For its first two seasons, *The Ann Sothern Show* aired after *The Danny Thomas Show* on Monday nights. In fall 1960, it was moved to Thursday nights up against Desilu's *The Untouchables* and was canceled at the end of its third season.

The Lucy Show

Before Lucille Ball starred on *The Lucy Show*, Desilu thought about making a special starring Lucy and Ann Sothern based on the book *Life without George* that was used as the basis for Lucy's second comedy series. This project was considered in September 1961 one year before *The Lucy Show* premiered.in October 1962.

Written by Irene Kampen about the consequences of her divorce from her husband George, the book related the story of Ms. Kampen and her friend, also a divorcee, sharing a house near Danbury, Connecticut with a child apiece and two Siamese cats. The book related incidents of two divorced women tackling issues like shoveling snow each winter, coping with the encroachment of sumac on the lawn, having a basement full of water, and participating in the local theater group.

In adapting the book for Lucy's second comedy, the Siamese cats were deleted, Lucy's character, Lucy Carmichael, was presented as a widow and not a divorcee, and she had two kids – not one. Vivian Vance played Lucy's housemate who was a divorcee raising one child.

Desi Arnaz was the executive producer of the series until he left the company in November 1962. Referring to his ex-wife's second series, Arnaz said, "I knew that CBS wanted her back on the air on a regular basis. So I had the book adapted into a TV series. And I got all the writers who wrote the *I Love Lucy show* – Bob Carroll, Madelyn Martin, Bob Weiskopf and Bob Schiller. And of course I had no trouble selling the show. I made a deal for three years with General Foods and Lever Brothers."[10]

Lucille Ball continued to play her Lucy Ricardo character on *The Lucy Show* – just with a new last name and no Ricky Ricardo or Fred Mertz. As a matter of fact, Jess Oppenheimer, who had produced *I Love Lucy*, sued Desilu and CBS for royalties from *The Lucy Show* claiming that the series used material from Ball's first television comedy.

During its six seasons, the comedy went through several cast changes. Gale Gordon, as banker Theodore J. Mooney, came on board in the second season. Vivian Vance left the series as a regular after the end of the 1964-65 season along with Ralph Hart, the actor who played Sherman, her son as did Candy Moore and Jimmy Garrett, the actors who appeared as Lucy's kids. *The Lucy Show* went from being a sitcom about a widowed mother and her best friend to one dealing with a single career woman frustrating her boss, Mr. Mooney.

During the series run, Lucille Ball contemplated changes to its overall format so she could play a character other than "Lucy." The possible formats ranged from Ms. Ball casting herself as a production company president and television actress as she was in real-life (something she attempted in a 1964 special with Bob Hope) to playing a wealthy, Carole-Lombard-like dress designer to having her character inherit a magazine company with Gale Gordon as the company's managing director and her character becoming involved in each of the magazine's departments.[11]

The Lucy Show came to an end when Desilu was sold to Gulf and Western Industries causing Lucille Ball to develop a new series, *Here's Lucy*, made by her own self-titled production company.

Chapter 2: Desi's Unsold Funny Lady Pilots

Certain of the following unsold comedy pilots starring actresses bore similarities to *I Love Lucy*, while some were more like the other sitcoms from Desilu described in the first chapter.

Just Off Broadway

Before entertainer Rose Marie became Sally Rogers on *The Dick Van Dyke Show*, she appeared as Rosemarie Warren along with Peggy Ryan playing her sister Peggy in this 1955 show business comedy initiative. The sisters rent an apartment in New York City to attempt to break into the big-time.

Moving into the apartment, Rosemarie finds Ray Mason (Ray McDonald), its current tenant, still living there. As coincidences happen, Ray, an amateur song plugger and professional dancer, has been trying to contact Rosemarie to perform songs from the music publisher for which he works. Also, as luck would have it, Peggy Warren is a dancer just like Ray, and Ray needs a dancing partner. Rosemarie has a job performing at a local nightclub. Ray's agent has landed a job for Ray and Peggy to perform free at a benefit, but they can only dance at the event if Rosemarie joins them. But her bosses at the club will not permit her to sing for free. Ray and Peggy go to the benefit anyway and are to perform as the last act. Rosemarie shows up and goes on as the final act. After Rosemarie apologizes to her sister and Ray, they do their number for her.

Just Off Broadway was initially called *Ring Around the Rosie* and also *Girls in Greasepaint*.

Adventures of a Model

Created by Sidney Sheldon and produced and directed by Norman Tokar, this comedy pilot, made in March 1956, featured Joanne Dru as career girl, Marilyn Woods – a model. Co-starring with Dru were William Redfield, as her doctor boyfriend – Dr. Boone, John Emery as Carter, the head of the agency for whom Woods worked, and Nancy Kulp as Aggie, Carter's secretary.

The pilot's story line had Marilyn receiving an assignment to model sportswear for a Mr. Hunter who is seeking an athletic female to become "Miss Huntress." Reluctantly, Marilyn attempts to pretend she is athletic resulting in "Lucy-like" physical comedy stunts. She plays golf but falls in a water hazard. Next, Marilyn tries archery but holds on to the arrow and launches the bow. She then attempts horseback riding. Realizing that she is not really an athlete, Mr. Hunter wants her to ride a gentle horse. By mistake, she takes a fast horse which gallops away resulting in her hanging from the limb of a tall tree. In the end, she confesses that she is not suited for outdoor activities. But, because she showed real spirit, she is hired to model Hunter's sports clothes line using her non-athletic style as the approach to the campaign.

Lucy and Desi appear at the end of the pilot talking with Joanne Dru and welcoming her to the Desilu family. At one point in 1956, the pilot appears to have actually been sold to Procter and Gamble for a CBS Saturday 9:30 time slot, but then the network balked at the deal and never turned it into a series.

In early 1957, when Arnaz announced that *I Love Lucy* would no longer air as a weekly thirty-minute series but instead, beginning in fall 1957 would become a periodic one-hour special, Desi wanted *The Adventures of a Model* to replace *I Love Lucy* on Mondays at 9:00. However, CBS decided to place *The Danny Thomas Show* in that time slot beginning with the 1957-58 season.

After airing in August 1958 as part of *Colgate Theatre*, *Variety* quipped, ". . . the plot meanders for 30 minutes through some entirely unlikely situations in which Miss Dru, a model pits her wits and curves against a series of wolfish suitors. The whole little more than a series of gag lines and situations, and most of the gags are of the creaky variety, but, accepted as the pure froth it is, the show amounts to something less than painful."[12]

Ernestine

In November 1957, Arnaz began developing a series for Marie Wilson who had previously starred on the comedy *My Friend, Irma* as a scatter-brained blonde. The series concept was to have the Marie Wilson character, Ernestine McDougall, work in a loan office and become involved with the problems of clients seeking money. Perhaps foreshadowing the relationship between Lucy Carmichael and Mr. Mooney on *The Lucy Show*, Ernestine had a soft heart and was willing to lend money to clients without any collateral. Desi had hoped that Gale Gordon would play her boss, but ultimately character actor Charles Lane was hired for the role of office manager, Morton Evans, in a company owned by Ernestine's father played by Charles Ruggles. Also, in the cast was Nancy Kulp as Mabel, the office assistant. The pilot, made in March 1958, was written by Don Nelson and Jay Sommers and directed by Sidney Salkow.

The test show had Ernestine wanting widow Mrs. Munson (Madge Blake), a tenant in the apartment building where Ernestine lives, to marry Ernestine's father. But, as typical of 1950s comedies starring females, instead of simply introducing her dad to the woman directly, Ernestine comes up with a scheme to have her dad unintentionally meet Mrs. Munson.

Ernestine's father brings Morton Evans to dinner at her apartment where she has purposely made a bad meal so her father will accept a dinner invitation from Mrs. Munson. After sampling Ernestine's soup which Evans likes but her father detests, Evans leaves. Mr. MacDougall and Ernestine then go to Mrs. Munson's place for beef stew. Ernestine leaves so that the two can be alone. MacDougall says he wants to "propose" which Ernestine, eavesdropping at the door, and Mrs. Munson interpret as a marriage proposal but which MacDougal meant as a toast. In the end, the building's superintendent proposes marriage to Mrs. Munson.

Although Arnaz approved of the concept for the series, the pilot was not to everyone's liking and much reshooting was needed. The revised pilot was screened in February 1959 with no takers wanting to turn it into a series.

Desi started working on another vehicle for the talents of Marie Wilson in late 1959. The initial concept was to pair her with actress Jacqueline McKeever as her cousin. Charlie Ruggles would have also played her father in this comedy attempt. *The Marie Wilson Show* would have had the actress working in a bookshop, but by May 1960, the idea was abandoned with no pilot being made.

All about Barbara

Created by *Lucy* writers, Madelyn Pugh Martin and Bob Carroll, Jr. and produced by Madelyn Martin's husband at the time, Quinn Martin, this comedy, about a famous Broadway musical comedy star who marries an English professor, was once contemplated as a vehicle for Lucille Ball after the end of the half-hour *I Love Lucy* series.

Desi Arnaz considered Marilyn Maxwell for the lead character, but Quinn Martin wanted blonde actress Barbara Nichols to star along with William Bishop as her husband. Reportedly, Quinn Martin had an affair with Nichols which led to Madelyn Pugh Martin divorcing him.

Barbara Nichols and William Bishop, the stars of the unsold pilot All about Barbara.

Larry Keating and Bea Benaderet, who had played husband and wife and the neighbors on *The George Burns and Gracie Allen Show*, co-starred in the pilot. Originally titled *All about Abby*, the concept of the planned series was to show how a free-spirited comic actress adapts to the staid environment of a small-town college married to a strait-laced professor.

In the pilot, Barbara has to fend off the advances of the college dean (Keating) while dealing with the snobbishness of his wife (Benaderet).

The premise for the planned series was the reverse of *I Love Lucy* with, instead of a homemaker who wants a career in show business, the Barbara character tries to give up her career in the entertainment world to become a housewife.

This comedy pilot was very similar to one that producer Quinn Martin attempted to launch in the late 1950s at Desilu starring Jane Russell. In 1958, newspapers reported that the actress was interested in a TV project to be called *Don't Blame Jane*. The series would have focused on a former show girl (Russell) who marries a college professor and has to adjust to life in a small town.

Gussie, My Girl

Arnaz had wanted to do a comedy starring Janis Paige for a number of years, and in 1960, he got his chance. He made a deal with Madelyn Pugh, whose last name was now "Davis," and Bob Carroll, Jr. to write the pilot and six scripts for a father/daughter, show business sitcom. Problems with casting the father role apparently postponed filming of the pilot until summer 1961. Actors Jack Oakie, James Dunn, and Frank McHugh were considered for the role of the father which finally went to vaudevillian Hank Henry.

The premise of the proposed series focused on Gussie, the youngest daughter of a show business family. Her parents had been in the business along with Gussie and her three sisters. After the mother died, the father put together a singing group with his four daughters and managed the act. When each of her sisters married, they left the act leaving now only Gussie and her dad.

When this initial pilot didn't sell, Desi Arnaz attempted to bring it back later in the 1960s when he formed his own production company. See Chapter 20 for more details.

Always April

Written by Bob Van Scoyk, directed by Richard Whorf, and co-produced by Desilu and Anso, this potential spinoff from *The Ann Sothern Show* starred Susan Silo, Constance Bennett, and John Emery. The back-door pilot, continuing the show business theme of many Desilu projects, involved the adventures of aspiring young actress April Fleming, the daughter of a retired show business couple Guinevere Lang and David Fleming.

Ann Sothern and Constance Bennett from Always April, a proposed back-door pilot from The Ann Sothern Show. *(Photo from the files of United Press International)*

In the pilot, Katy O'Conner discovers a girl living in room 1022 at the Bartley House hotel whom she thinks is destitute because she has been eating only peanut butter. April explains to Katy that she has run away from school to be an actress. Katy calls her parents in Vermont. Initially, her mother, Guinevere doesn't believe that her daughter is in New York, but then realizes that Katy may be right. She and her husband go to the city to pick up their daughter. Although April seeks to stay in New York to pursue acting, her dad doesn't want her to become an actress. Katy suggests that her father, who now raises sugar maple trees in Vermont, should sit in on April's acting class to see if she has any talent. Katy and the parents go to the class where, at the direction of the teacher played by Leonid Kinskey, April and Erskine Wild (Marty Ingels) act out a scene from *The Taming of the Shrew* done with a Brooklyn accent. When April's mother reveals that she has been couching her daughter, the parents go on stage to demonstrate how the scene should really be performed. After April replaces her mother in the scene, her dad agrees that she has talent to become an actress. April returns to Vermont with them since her mother has allowed the acting class to use their barn as a summer theater. The episode aired Feb. 23, 1961.

Pandora

This proposed spin-off from *The Ann Sothern Show* was broadcast on March 16, 1961. Starring Pat Carroll, the episode was written by John Fenton Murray and Benedict Freedom and directed by Richard Whorf.

In the back-door pilot, Carroll played Pandora Peterson who has just left her small town and moved to Hollywood. Katy O'Connor, who happens to be visiting friends in Hollywood, calls an employment agency to hire a secretary for movie star Tony Bardot (Luke Anthony). Katy gets klutzy Pandora who turns out to be an excellent typist, but swoons when she is introduced to her boss, Tony. Tony's chauffeur, Gabby (Guy Mitchell) instructs Pandora to make sure she keeps the door to the house locked so that when he and his boss are out, no fans break in. When a sightseeing bus comes by and one of the passengers gets off to take some pictures, the passenger, who is a big fan of Tony Bardot, lays down on the doormat. Thinking that the woman has fallen, Pandora invites her in followed by the rest of the bus passengers who loot the house for souvenirs. Bardot comes home and is mobbed. He fires Pandora, but, before she leaves, she tells him that he is not neighborly and not handsome. Liking Pandora's honesty, he rehires her.

This spin-off came about because Pat Carroll had done an episode of *Private Secretary* titled "Susie for President" where the Ann Sothern character runs for president of the Midtown Secretaries League. The two actresses worked well together on the episode, and Sothern proposed a spin-off series for Carroll.

Oh, Nurse

Writer Phil Shuken prepared a script for a hospital comedy in August 1962. The planned series was to star Glynis Johns who later had the title role in the short-lived Desilu comedy, *Glynis*.

Johns played Nurse Jane Cotton at Bryant General Hospital. Her colleague and friend at the hospital is Martha "Marty" Richmond. Jane holds a party for the hospital's doctors who have completed their residencies. The next day a whole new group of residents arrive. Each nurse is assigned a resident to introduce them to the hospital's patients for whom they will be caring. Jane gets Dr. Stickney, a surgeon who will be performing his first operation on a nervous gall bladder patient. Jane assures the patient that everything will be all right, but Dr. Stickney, not interested in Jane's advice, orders her out of the room which angers Jane.

Later, Jane learns that the nervous patient has asked for another doctor to perform his surgery. On the morning of the planned operation, Stickney hears that he has been replaced. He decides to resign from the hospital's staff but changes his mind when he is scheduled to perform another surgery. This time he asks Jane for advice on how to handle the patient. The patient turns out to be Jane herself who needs to have her appendix removed.

In many respects, this comedy pilot was similar to *The Ann Sothern Show*. Like the Ann Sothern character, Jane Cotton was a professional woman who oftentimes knew better than the men she encountered in her workaday life.

During his tenure as Desilu president, Arnaz had meetings with other female celebrities about starring in shows for his company. In 1958, he offered Rhonda Fleming a chance to do a series, but she declined saying being on television would end her movie career. In 1960, it was reported that singer Patti Page had plans to do a comedy series at Desilu, but no such pilot or series ever resulted from those plans.

Chapter 3: Desi's Unsold Funny Guys Pilots

Unlike the successful female-centric comedies produced under Desi Arnaz's management, the company couldn't seem to sell a comedy series with a male central character despite numerous attempts.

Eddie Quillan Project

Arnaz contemplated developing a comedy series starring vaudeville and movie actor/singer, Eddie Quillan as a possible summer replacement for *I Love Lucy* in 1953. While little information is available about this project, apparently the series may have been based on the novels by Frank Gruber featuring an inept amateur detective called Johnny Fletcher.

In addition to the Gruber books and at least one movie, *The French Key* (1946) starring Albert Dekker as Fletcher, ABC began airing the Fletcher mysteries on radio in 1948. Brief mentions in some newspapers in 1953 indicate that Quillan would star as a private eye in a TV series called *The Adventures of Johnny Fletcher*.

Ritz Brothers

In September 1956, Desilu was planning a series premise for the Ritz Brothers in which they would play themselves in real and varied situations and locales. The Ritz Brothers – Al, Jimmy, and Harry, were an old-style vaudeville team who sang, danced, and performed boisterous, manic comedy routines.

Dick Mack was preparing a script for the pilot. Desilu hoped that it could do for the Ritz Brothers what the Bilko characterization did for Phil Silvers.

Evidently nothing came of this initiative.

The Bob Hope Show

Desi Arnaz discussed the possibility of legendary comedian Bob Hope starring on his own comedy produced by Desilu. This late 1956 project came about after a meeting with Hope and Arnaz over Desilu filming a pilot produced by Hope called *The Police Hall of Fame*. Hope thought of making what was labeled a sitcom about the armed services after realizing the income that could be earned in the form of residuals from reruns of a successful show. Although having appeared on television almost from its inception, the comedian's live and kinescoped specials were not considered rerun potential like a filmed series would have been. However, no series resulted from this possibility.

Sad Sack

In summer 1957, Desilu thought of developing an Army comedy starring Tom Ewell and co-starring Arnold Stang to be produced by George Baker. Sgt. George Baker had created the *Sad Sack* comic strip while in the Army during World War II. The strip portrayed the trials and tribulations of a lowly private.

No pilot was ever made. But in 1957, Jerry Lewis did star in a motion picture based on the comic strip.

Night Watchman

Max Baer, whose son, Max Baer Jr. later starred as Jethro on *The Beverly Hillbillies*, was a former boxer and television personality in the 1950s. In 1958, Desi Arnaz attempted to come up with a comedy vehicle for Baer, Sr's talents wherein the former pugilist would play a night watchman. Three months after the idea was proposed, it was canceled in May 1958.

Where There's Smokey

Before he was Mr. Mooney on *The Lucy Show*, Gale Gordon starred on this pilot as fire chief Warren Packard whose brother-in-law, Smokey Stevens played by Milton "Soupy" Sales, appeared as a bumbling fireman reporting to the chief. The town in which they lived had not had a fire in ten years. The interaction between Warren and Smokey was similar to how Mr. Mooney acted toward Lucy's antics.

Smokey lived in a room above Packard's garage and helped around the Packard household by babysitting his nephew, Richie (Ricky Allen), and doing various other household chores. Warren Packard's wife (Smokey's sister) was named Blossom (Hollis Irving), and Smokey had a girlfriend, Maggie Dennison (Louise Glenn), who was a school teacher.

In the pilot made in early 1959, Smokey is going to a wedding with Maggie. The other firemen think that Maggie is trying to rope Smokey into proposing to her. Wanting Smokey to move out, Warren initially tries to convince him to marry, but then, after talking with his wife about all the things Smokey does around the house, Warren changes course and attempts to talk him out of marriage. Smokey makes his mind up to inform Maggie he doesn't want to marry her. To his surprise, she agrees. He later has second thoughts and reconsiders marriage. Maggie says that she will only consider marriage if he stands up to his brother-in-law whom she thinks takes advantage of him. While Smokey tries to stand up to Warren, the fire chief, based on his wife's ultimatum, ends up apologizing to Smokey.

Rod Amateau, who had directed several episodes of *The George Burns and Gracie Allen Show*, produced and directed this pilot as well as possessing an ownership interest in the property.

Aldo Ray Project

Desi Arnaz became personally involved in coming up with a situation comedy for actor Aldo Ray. Ray had co-starred as a boxer in "K. O. Kitty," an installment of *Desilu Playhouse* that included a rare appearance by Lucille Ball playing a character other than her Lucy persona. On that episode, Aldo Ray's character, a fighter, decides to leave boxing and become a farmer. Unknown is if this planned comedy would feature Ray in a continuation of the same role he portrayed on "K. O. Kitty" or in a different role. In any event, two months after initiating the project, it was canceled in December 1960.

My Wife's Brother

The concept of this pilot was very much like *Where There's Smokey*, described above, dealing with a husband and his brother-in-law living with him and his wife. The comedy team of Rowan and Martin were tapped for the pilot written by Cy Howard and Henry Garson.

Lucille Ball's protégé from the Desilu Workshop, Carole Cook, played the wife of the Dan Rowan character and the sister of the Dick Martin character. Filmed in early 1961 for ABC, the planned series was earmarked for the 1961-62 TV season.

Before appearing on the hit *Laugh-In* with Dan Rowan that competed against *Here's Lucy* on Monday nights, Dick Martin co-starred on the first season of *The Lucy Show* as Harry Connors, Lucy Carmichael's next-door neighbor.

College Humor

Desilu, in conjunction with Frank Sinatra's Essex Productions, sought to develop a musical situation comedy, *College Humor*, in early 1962 with the campus of UCLA as the background. The planned series was to star three of Bing Crosby's sons – Dennis, Lindsay, and Phillip Crosby. Lindsay was to portray an undergraduate student with Phillip and Dennis as his older brothers running a nearby men's clothing store. Reportedly, the project was scuttled because of Lindsay Crosby's poor health at the time. Lindsay had suffered a nervous breakdown over the death of his child born prematurely.

Swingin' Together

Written by Howard Leeds, this 1962 project starred singer Bobby Rydell as the leader of a band called Bobby Day and His Four Knights. The Four Knights were Ben Bryant as Scooby-Doo, Larry Merrill as Steve, Peter Brooks as Yogi, and Art Metrano as Big D.

The test show concerned the band's manager and bus driver, P.J. Cunningham (James Dunn), booking the musicians to perform at a charity dance organized by Linda Craig (Stephanie Powers). Before they perform, Ms. Craig fires them stating that they do not fit the charity's image. Linda's father apologizes to P.J. for his daughter's behavior and guarantees that the band will play despite Linda's objections. Bobby and his band perform "The Start of Something Big" to the delight of the crowd. After the number, Bobby converses with Linda who still doesn't like the band, but then she decides to join the rest of the crowd dancing to "Let's Twist Again."

The project started out in fall 1961 as *The Bobby Rydell Show* and was subsequently changed to *Teenage Millionaire*. *Teenage Millionaire* was a

1961 movie starring singer Jimmy Clanton as Bobby Schultz, who goes to live with his wealthy aunt after his parents die. At a radio station owned by his aunt, he records a song which is circulated by a girl he meets, and the song becomes popular. The initial idea for ABC was for Rydell to play Bobby Schultz with Judy Rawlins as his girlfriend. In December 1961, the concept was changed with Rydell now leading a rock 'n' roll group and the title became *Saturday Nights* before changing to *Swingin' Together*.

Although having a show business theme like several other Desilu pilots at the time, this project represented a rare venture into rock and roll music for the studio.

Chapter 4: Desi's Unsold Funny Couples Pilots

Besides making Lucille Ball a television legend, *I Love Lucy* can also be defined as a "couple's comedy" based on the interactions between Lucy and Ricky and Fred and Ethel. Under Arnaz's leadership, Desilu attempted several funny couple's comedies with only three – *Guestward Ho!*, *Harrigan and Son*, and *Fair Exchange* ever becoming series. *Fair Exchange* began development when Desi was president of the company but premiered when Lucy became the head of Desilu.

For the most part, the unsold pilots in this chapter deal with two or three main characters, either related by family or else by friendship.

The Rolling Stones

First proposed in November 1955, this comedy planned to cover the experiences and adventures of Nathaniel Stone and his grand-daughter, Sheila, as they travel around the country in a trailer. Robert Dennis came up with the concept and the script.

Actor Charles Coburn was initially considered for the role of the granddad. Later, in 1956, Rudy Vallee and Margaret O'Brien were signed for the roles. No pilot was ever produced.

You're Only Young Twice

This proposed comedy began development in late 1957 with Ralph Bellamy and Myrna Loy considered for the leads in a vehicle about the adventures of a married couple in their late forties whose grown children are married. The husband is virtually retired and wants to relax, while his wife seeks fun and activity. *I Love Lucy* writers, Bob Schiller and Bob Weiskopf, wrote the original scripts for the project.

In early 1958, still trying to cast the pilot, Joan Blondell was sought for the role of the wife with casting still underway for an actor to play the husband. Melvyn Douglas was reportedly to fill that role with Blondell, but by December 1958, George Murphy was tapped to play the husband with Joan Bennett as a possibility for the wife. In early 1959, Bennett was no longer under consideration for the role. Murphy was trying to get Irene Dunne or Jeanette MacDonald to be his wife in the pilot. Finally, by March 1959, the pilot was filmed with George Murphy and Martha Scott playing the husband and wife.

The pilot focused on how Charles (Murphy) and Kit Tyler (Scott) are coping with retirement. The couple has a maid named Olga (Jane Darwell) who encourages both of them to have a good time. Kit wants to travel, but Charles is happy staying at home. Their daughter Louise suggests going on a second honeymoon to a hotel located near the beach. Louise, her husband Arthur, and their young child accompany Charles and Kit to the Carlton Inn. At the hotel, Kit and Charles dance and have dinner. They run into Ronny and Gloria. Charles had been an insurance agent, and Ronny was one of his clients, while Gloria is Kit's friend. When Gloria asks Charles if he wants to dance, Kit becomes jealous. Unbeknownst to Kit, Charles receives a phone call from Louise asking him to babysit his grandchild. Back at the hotel room, Charles is talking to the child when Kit returns thinking that Charles has brought Gloria back to their room. Visibly upset, Kit storms in only to see Charles holding their grandchild.

In addition to starring on this pilot, George Murphy was a Desilu vice president from 1958 to 1961 and later became a U.S. Senator from California.

The Mertzes

Desi Arnaz came up with the idea in 1958 for a spin-off staring Vivian Vance and William Frawley as Ethel and Fred Mertz who were the Ricardo's neighbors on *I Love Lucy*. However, Desi's plan for such a spin-off was opposed by Vance who refused to appear with irascible William Frawley in any series without Lucy and Desi.[13]

The two co-stars of *I Love Lucy* never really had a good working relationship. As described in the book, *Meet the Mertzes*, Vance rejected the idea of a spin-off with Frawley,

> ... because she could not stomach the notion of costarring on an even more full-time basis with a man as crude

Vivian Vance and William Frawley otherwise known as Ethel and Fred Mertz. Off screen, they had a frosty relationship, but they were all smiles for publicity photos.

and insulting as she found Frawley to be. She would not film a pilot episode – even after Desi Arnaz agreed to pay her a $50,000 bonus. (Supposedly, Vance came up with the $50,000 amount to compensate for the $450 she made for each episode of *I Love Lucy* during its initial seasons.) When Frawley learned of Vance's refusal, he was irate, if only because the eternally money-conscious actor – who had a well-earned reputation as a cheapskate – would have been paid a much-higher salary than he currently was earning. [14]

One might speculate about the premise of a Mertzes spin-off. During the later episodes of *I Love Lucy*, the characters of Fred and Ethel had moved to Connecticut to live in the guest house on the Ricardo's property. Fred was in charge of raising chickens but still owned the apartment building in New York City which was being managed by Mrs. Trumble. If the idea of a spin-off had been developed, it could have involved Fred and Ethel moving back to the city to resume managing their apartment building and dealing with the problems of their tenants. Perhaps, a new couple would have moved into the apartment vacated by the Ricardo's with the Mertzes taking them under their wing.

Guestward Ho!

This comedy, based on the book of the same title written by Barbara Hooton and Patrick Dennis, went through several cast changes but, unlike the other pilots profiled in this work, it did eventually become a series.

Starting in 1956, Eve Arden was suggested as the star of this project about a New York couple who buys a dude ranch sight unseen and moves across country to operate it. By 1957, CBS sought Jeanne Crain for the pilot, but, when this casting didn't work out, the network abandoned the project.

In April 1958, Desilu bought the property from CBS with the idea of fashioning the planned series for Vivian Vance. In November of that year, Desi announced a co-production deal for the series with CBS. Bob Schiller and Bob Weiskopf were writing the pilot script and Ralph Levy, who had worked on *The George Burns and Gracie Allen Show* as well as *The Jack Benny Program*, would produce the series. Vance's husband at the time, Phil Ober, who had appeared as MGM executive Dore Schary on the *I Love Lucy* episodes set in Hollywood, lobbied his wife to ask Desi Arnaz to play her husband in the pilot. But Desi would not consider him.[15] Hugh Marlowe was tested for that role, but the part went to Leif Erikson. A pilot was made in March 1959.

In the pilot, Bill Hooten (Erikson) informs his wife Babs (Vance) that he has taken out a lease on the Rancho de la Vista in Santa Fe, New Mexico. Babs points out that they know nothing about ranching, but she decides to go with her husband across country. The couple meets the ranch staff – Don "Snag" Anderson (Ray Hemphill), the wrangler; Rita (Bella Bruck), the housekeeper; and a cook. Bill and Babs witness several guests fleeing the ranch and find that they are leaving fearing a mountain lion in the area who has been evading the traps set for it. The cook informs Bill that there is no lion and that Snag has been stealing the bait for himself. Bill encounters more problems when he can't pay the staff because the ranch has no guests. Bill enlists the cook to help him dig a pit to trap either the mountain lion or Snag. When later Babs goes for a late-night walk with her dog, Gilbert, she falls into the pit and is outraged to find that there may be a mountain lion on the loose. After she returns home, she sees the lion and manages to trap it in the bedroom. Babs receives a reward for capturing the animal from the Santa Fe Ranch Association. Bill and Babs are pleased when their first guests arrive – and drive right into the pit.

When the pilot didn't sell, Desilu considered redoing it with a new cast. A new script was done by Ron Alexander with Jerry Thorpe directing. The stars were now Joanne Dru and Mark Miller. This version finally did become a series on ABC and lasted for one season.

Three in a Row

This 1959 to 1960 project, if it had become a series, would have been the first regular weekly one-hour situation comedy. Created by Cy Howard, the concept concerned three neighboring households – two families and a bachelor and their interactions among each other. The project was tied to ABC, but no pilot resulted from the premise.

Cy Howard, who had created comedies like *My Friend, Irma*, had been hired by Desilu to develop comedy pilots for the studio. Signed to a five-year-contract, a few years after *Three in a Row*, Howard did launch a one-hour Desilu comedy on CBS, *Fair Exchange*, about a British family and an American one who exchange daughters for a year.

Cloud Nine

Created by John W. Loveton and written by Bob Schiller and Bob Weiskopf, this 1960 proposal was a fantasy comedy in the vein of *Topper* which Loveton had produced. Since *Topper* was a sitcom about husband and wife ghosts interfering in the life of banker Cosmo Topper, one could speculate, based on the title of this proposal, that it may have concerned angels from on high becoming involved in the lives of mere mortals.

If the project had advanced, it would have been a departure for Desi Arnaz from the more traditional sitcom formats described in this chapter.

Man of Letters

A comedy-adventure project considered by Desilu in late 1960 concerned a wealthy father and his nerdish son. The father character is a fun-loving, free-spirited individual; his son is just the opposite. The half-hour pilot script, "The General," was written by Ed Adamson and Norman Katkov.

Jeremiah Kimble II is the conservative, opinionated son of Jerry Kimble. Both live in a mansion with an elderly housekeeper named Emma. One day Jeremiah reads in the local paper that Founder's Circle will be turned into a parking lot. Outraged, he types a letter to the editor of the paper objecting to the plan. He then attends a council meeting where the parking lot proposal is on the agenda. The meeting is open to the public, but only Jeremiah is there. The council chair, Marjorie Franklin, and the other council members listen to his case, but vote to go forth with the plan. Jeremiah next stages a sit-in on the statue of the town's founder, the General and his horse.

His sit-in lasts for nine days and elicits coverage by the local TV station. A large truck then arrives to remove the statue from the circle. The statue is pulled up a ramp onto the flat bed of the truck with Jeremiah still sitting on it. He and the statue are placed in a warehouse. His father Jerry comes by to take his defeated son home. He praises his son's efforts for fighting the good fight. Marjorie visits Jeremiah, and they go to a nearby park where the statue has been relocated. She kisses him, but his attention is turned elsewhere. He sees that the statue is facing South instead of North where it was originally situated. Disturbed by this, he sends another letter to the editor.

No pilot based on the script was ever made. However, in the same year – 1960, Desilu did launch a comedy, *Harrigan and Son*, with a similar theme of a liberal father and a conservative son. Starring Pat O'Brien as James Harrigan, Sr. and Roger Perry as James Harrigan, Jr., the comedy about two lawyers involved the son doing everything by the book while the father played it fast and loose in winning his cases.

Phil Harris/Alice Faye Show

Beginning in late 1960, Desi Arnaz attempted to put together a family comedy starring Phil Harris and his wife Alice Faye. At one point, Bing Crosby's sons, Phillip, Lindsay, and Dennis Crosby, were reportedly considered for playing the couple's offspring. A treatment was written for the show by Ray Singer and Dick Chevillat, who had scripted the Harris/Faye radio series. However, the pilot for NBC was never made.

Presumably, the television series would have been similar in format to the radio program which was really a "show within a show." On radio, Harris and Faye played themselves as entertainers living at home with their children and working on a radio show. Phil Harris was portrayed as a singer and orchestra leader with Alice Faye as a vocalist. Much of the humor made fun of Harris' persona as a heavy drinker and Faye his supportive wife.

You Can't Win Them All

Based on baseball player Jim Brosnan's book, *The Long Season*, Bob Schiller and Bob Weiskopf wrote a script for this proposed family comedy. While the planned series did not focus on baseball per se, the father figure was a pitcher for the Cincinnati Reds.

Brosnan had been a Major League pitcher for nine years before he went on to be a sportscaster and writer. He played for the St. Louis Cardinals, Chicago Cubs, and Chicago White Sox in addition to the Cincinnati Reds. *The Long Season* was an account of his career as a pitcher in 1959. While the book dealt mostly with the game, elements of it could lend themselves to a family comedy. Brosnan was married to Anne Stewart who for reasons best left to the reader's imagination nicknamed him "Meat." The Brosnan's had two children – Jamie and Tim.

In one section of the book, he describes packing a station wagon to get ready for a family road trip:

> We were supposed to hit the road at six A.M., and we set a new family record by leaving only one hour and forty minutes late. Packing a car with two kids, a dozen toys, and enough clothes for a two months' trip takes special training. Although we must do it half a dozen times a year it is an exhausting, sometimes frustrating job.
>
> A dozen suitcases, grips, bags, and boxes can be quickly and neatly stacked between the driver's seat and the kids. But, invariably, I end up with this huge hatbox outside on the ground, looking like a lost carburetor. "Why in hell do you need a boxful of hats?" I'd ask. "For six years I've wrestled with this thing!"
>
> "You never know when you may need them," my wife would reply.
>
> "There's one hat in here you haven't worn since we've been married."

"Put it in the car, Meat." [16]

By February 1961, Desilu shelved the project.

The Holidays Abroad

Produced in early 1961, this Desilu pilot, starring Dan Duryea and Maggie Hayes, dealt with the career of a newspaperman who wonders through Europe doing his job accompanied by his family – wife, son, and daughter. Created by Josef Shaftel and Stanley Adams, based on a script by Bill Manhoff, the pilot was for ABC.

Sam Holiday (Duryea), a famous syndicated columnist, travels throughout America gathering material for his columns. His wife Dorie (Hayes) and his two children – Susan (Taffy Paul), age sixteen, and ten-year-old Henry (Barry Gordon), dislike that he is away so much. Dorie even threatens to divorce him. Hearing Sam's complaints about not being with his family, his boss, Harrison, decides to send Sam to Europe to do his stories and allow him to take his family with him at company expense.

Sam's first assignment in Europe will be to interview reclusive French author Henri Valois. The family is thrilled about going to Europe and busily prepare to leave. After a week of packing, they fly to Paris and settle in their new apartment. While his family goes sightseeing, Sam tries to track down Valois. Susan meets a young French teen. At a café at night with Susan, the teen sees Valois at the next table. Susan phones her father to meet her at the café for a surprise, but Sam is upset that she is out so late. When Sam and Dorie arrive at the café, he lectures her unaware that Valois is nearby. Valois says that Sam is acting like a fool. Sam responds that the man should mind his own business. They get into a brief altercation before Susan explains who the man at the adjacent table is. After trading more insults, Valois relents to an interview with Sam.

Subsequent to the pilot being filmed, writers Bob Schiller and Bob Weiskopf suggested some changes to various scenes. For example, in the final scene at the café, after the phone call from Susan, Schiller and Weiskopf recommended that Dorie go alone to the café. She then phones her husband to come to the café. When he does, he sees his wife, Susan, the French boy, and Valois sitting together and thinks that Dorie has been picked up by this fellow at the table. But Dorie and Susan proudly proclaim that they have been a big help to Sam in getting the interview with

Valois. Not known is whether any of the suggestions resulted in redoing any of the scenes.

Mickey and the Contessa

Mickey Shaughnessy starred with Eva Gabor in this 1961 pilot about a widowed athletic coach with two children who hires an immigrant domestic to care for his kids and ends up getting a real Contessa. Cy Howard and Mike Fessier scripted the ABC pilot with Howard producing along with William Asher.

The basketball team at Redwood College is in an uproar. The team didn't do well in the previous season and wants Coach Brennan (Shaughnessy) fired. Meanwhile, the Coach contacts a Hungarian employment agency to hire a "little old lady" to cook, clean, and take care of his two kids – tomboy Sissy (Ann Marshall) and chess-playing Bill (Bill St. John). Mickey Brennan goes to the train station to pick up his new housekeeper and finds that she is a very young and pretty woman, Contessa Czigoina, from a prestigious family in Hungry. The Contessa's aunt is the Duchess of Beverly Hills, and her cousin is the head of Hollywood Studios.

Back at the college, Brennan is trying to recruit a new member for the basketball team – Butch Gorky (Michael Greene). In testing Gorky's abilities at the sport, Brennan corrects his form and technique. Gorky becomes nervous and decides not to play. When the head of the school's board of trustees finds that Gorky quit the team, he threatens to fire the Coach. The Contessa, who has already reorganized the Brennan household and persuaded Sissy to start wearing dresses, learns about the situation with "24 point" Gorky and invites him to dinner at the Brennan's. Gorky and the Contessa bond over her cooking and the fact that both are of Hungarian descent. At dinner, Brennan tries to convince the boy to join the team. After the promise of more good food from the Contessa, Gorky decides to become a member of the basketball team.

The pilot aired on *Vacation Playhouse* on August 12, 1963.

The Two of Us

Desilu tried something different with this 1962 comedy pilot starring Patricia Crowley and Billy Mumy. The pilot combined live action and animation for a proposed series about a children's book illustrator (Crowley whose son (Mumy) fantasizes about the characters his mother draws.

Spanner

This September 1962 proposed comedy was about a father and daughter team who run a sports car service garage. Arnaz set Alan Armer as producer and Harry Kronman as writer of this project. It was abandoned by November 1962. In mid-1963, consideration was given to making this a one-hour drama, but no pilot resulted from this idea.

When Arnaz established his own production company later in the 1960s, he considered a project similar to this one called *Ham and Davey*. See Chapter 20 for more details.

Chapter 5: Desi's Purely Fictional Unsold Drama Attempts

In May 1955, Dave Kaufman announced in his *Variety* column, "Over at Desilu, home of 'I Love Lucy,' which initiated the situation comedy trend, the future plans include no situation comedies. Desi Arnaz, Martin Leeds, and (Desilu producer) Sam Marx huddled, decided to film action series, oaters, sea stories, etc., in the future."[17]

Like most television production companies at the time, Desilu tried to sell dramatic series of almost every genre.

Downbeat

As Desi Arnaz wrote in his autobiography, "In the early part of 1953, Frank Sinatra agreed to do a pilot for us called *Downbeat* . . . It was a story about a singer who had a small combo in New York and who would always get mixed up with broads and gangsters and all kinds of different intrigues in his struggle for success and often just plain survival. It was a kind of melodrama with generous portions of music and humor."[18] The proposed series was alternatively titled *Blues in the Night*.

A pilot script was written by Seymour Robinson and Stanley Raub. However, before filming could begin, Sinatra bowed out because he got what turned out to be his Oscar-winning role in the feature, *From Here to Eternity*.

For a period of time, Sinatra rented space from Desilu for his Essex Productions. But in April 1961, the singer decided to move his production headquarters from Desilu to the Sam Goldwyn Studios presumably over a feud with Arnaz about how certain ethnic groups were portrayed in the Desilu hit drama, *The Untouchables*. Evidently, what started as a discussion about how Italians were presented on the drama set during the Prohibition era almost ended up in fisticuffs.[19] This incident apparently did not end Desilu's cooperation with Essex Productions on other ventures since the two companies tried to launch *College Humor*, described above, with Bing Crosby's sons.

Fast Freight

This planned comedy-adventure series starring Keenan Wynn and Tom D'Andrea would deal with the exploits of two, long-haul, wise-cracking truck drivers, partners in an independent trucking firm. Desilu executive Martin Leeds had been trying to develop this project since 1954.

The project for ABC was abandoned in February 1957 due to casting problems. Keenan Wynn pulled out of the proposed series, and the network did not go for Jackie Coogan as one of the leads.

Country Doctor

Based on the works of A.J. Cronin, this 1954 half-hour drama pilot concerned a young medical school graduate, Scott Findley, played by Arthur Franz, who takes a job as an apprentice to Dr. Andrew Cameron (Charles Coburn), an old curmudgeonly doctor. The Cronin stories were set in Scotland, but the planned series changed the location to New England circa 1911. The pilot, "Chapter One – How It Began," told how the young doctor started practicing medicine in a small New England town. Dr. Findley, just having graduated from medical school, begins his career as a pharmacist's assistant and then receives an opportunity to work with Dr. Cameron at a low salary.

The pilot was William Spier's first project for Desilu. He had been hired by the company in April 1954 as a producer/director/writer.

Initially, Desi Arnaz wanted to film the show in front of a live audience like *I Love Lucy*, something rarely, if ever, done for a dramatic series. As Arnaz explained:

> We are taking the best of the live and the film techniques and combining them so that we'll get the maximum benefits from both. The chief fault of Hollywood's filmed dramatic shows today is that the actors, the director and so on have no time for rehearsal; they come in at the last minute, and the lack of rehearsal time shows on the screen. We will thoroughly rehearse every picture, then present it before the

live audience, so that we'll have the legit technique plus the advantages of film.[20]

However, the live audience idea was dropped when the pilot was made. After Desilu was unable to sell this pilot to a sponsor or the networks, syndicator National Telefilm Associates stepped in to try to have local stations purchase the series. While NTA was unable to do so, if the firm had been successful, this would have been Desilu's debut in the syndication market.

In 1955, Arnaz considered making a feature film based on the Cronin works, but that idea was abandoned.

Mr. Tutt

Made in May 1954 for CBS but not aired until September 10, 1958, this thirty-minute comedy-drama, based on the Arthur Train stories, featured Walter Brennan as a small-town lawyer with Olive Blakeney as his secretary, Minerva, and Harry Harvey Jr. as Charlie, his investigator.

The pilot involved Mr. Ephraim Tutt helping a girl, Judy Gregory (Vera Miles) who thought that her late grandfather was leaving a substantial sum to her to purchase equipment for a clinic at which she works. Tutt finds that the grandfather changed his will right before he died to make Judy's uncle the main beneficiary. Upon reviewing the latest will, Mr. Tutt sees that the uncle is listed as both the witness to the will as well as its chief beneficiary. At the probate hearing, Tutt points out that if the uncle testifies as a witness, he will forfeit his right as beneficiary. However, the uncle is nowhere to be found. The judge gives Tutt two weeks to locate him. He finds the uncle fishing in Vermont, near the New York state line. Tutt lures him back to New York using the ruse that he discovered a great fishing spot downstream which happens to be in New York state. Unbeknownst to the uncle, he wades downstream crossing the Vermont border into New York, and Tutt serves him with a subpoena ordering him to testify thereby giving up his right as main beneficiary to the estate.

Although this pilot never sold, a few years after it was made, Walter Brennan did get his own television series. In 1957, he starred as Grandpa Amos McCoy on *The Real McCoys* that ran for several seasons.

The Black Arrow

Based on the Robert Louis Stevenson book, in 1955 Desilu attempted to make a pilot called *The Black Arrow* set in the American West with an unknown actor in the lead. The planned series was created and written by Charles Smith and Ralph Rose.

The setting for the novel by Stevenson was the War of the Roses - a series of civil wars from 1453 to 1487 between the house of Lancaster and the house of York fighting for the English throne. The book related the tale of Dick Shelton chronicling how he became a knight, rescued his love interest, and obtained justice for the murder of his father. Shelton joins an outlaw group called the Black Arrows, whose weapons and calling cards are ebony arrows.

Presumably, the television adaptation would have featured a hero like Robin Hood avenging injustice in the Old West.

The Wildcatters

Mort Briskin worked to develop this 1956 project concerning two oil engineers traveling around the world – one of whom would be serious about his work with the other more interested in romance. Attempts were made to gain the endorsement of the American Petroleum Association for the planned series.

Actors Lance Fuller and Ken Clark played the leads in the pilot produced in association with NTA (National Telefilm Associates). Most of Desilu's syndicated series were made in coordination with National Telefilm Associates and most were helmed by Mort Briskin. NTA, founded by Ely Landau, distributed movies and series to over one hundred TV stations.

Rookie Cop

Desi Arnaz had hoped to interest Keenan Wynn into starring in this situation comedy/mystery hybrid. Lever Brothers indicated it might sponsor the series. The setting for this late 1956 project was to be Chicago, but filming would be done at the Desilu Studios.

Neither writers, directors, nor a starting production date were determined for the pilot, and on March 27, 1957, the project was dropped with no pilot made.

The Last Marshal

James Craig starred as a U.S. Marshal appointed by the Attorney General to maintain the peace in various Western territories during the 1880s. The Craig character comes to the aid of an ex-convict who has returned to his hometown to resume his life after serving his term for murder. The ex-con is about to be hanged for outdrawing the local sheriff, but the Marshal insists that he receive a fair trial.

Desilu filmed the pilot, written by Hugh King, in February 1957. The role of the marshal was originally to be played by Jim Davis (later of *Dallas* fame), but he had another film commitment and so was replaced by James Craig.

The potential series was earmarked for syndication.

Personal Report, Inc.

Created by Desilu executive Martin Leeds, this pilot involved two former FBI agents - Mike "Touch" Connors as Bradley Morton and Wayne Morris as Larry Blair, who now run a private detective agency. They file reports on individuals concerning any type of personal problem. Investigations ranged from murder to tracing the backgrounds of adopted children.

In the 1957 pilot, the two detectives take on the case of Chris Andrews, a young man discovered at the scene of the murder of Preston Wells. Andrews is caught holding a gun and is arrested for the murder. Chris' parents contact Morton and Blair to look into the case. Andrews refuses to defend himself thinking that he will take the blame for his fiancée, the dead man's sister, Diana, whom he believes actually killed her brother because he was against the marriage. Wells' law partner also contacts the two detectives to have them find out who really killed Preston Wells since he doesn't think either Chris or Diana committed the murder. Diana confides that, before her brother died, he told her that he would no longer object to the marriage. The detectives find that the day after he was killed, Wells was scheduled to meet with the FBI concerning his partner who was doing business with the Soviet Union. The partner killed Wells to cover up his shady dealings with the Communists.

If it had become s series, the plan was for the two leads to alternate every other week as the principal star in the episode, with both actors appearing jointly on every third show.

Mike Connors later starred as Joe Mannix in the Desilu-produced private detective drama *Mannix*.

Tonight in Havana

Fletcher Markle and David Ahler developed this 1957 adventure series in conjunction with Desilu and NTA. Starring Ricardo Montalban and Lita Milan, the planned series was based on *The Saturday Evening Post* stories of Burnham Carter about a young married couple running a café in Havana, Cuba.

The pilot had the Montalban character becoming involved in the case of a woman who is a refugee from both the Nazis and the Communists. The Communists had stolen some of her jewelry which the woman spots on a Russian female in Cuba. The woman asks the Montalban character to retrieve her necklace. Despite being shadowed by Cuban secret police, he is able to swipe the necklace.

As *Variety* wrote, "There is no question as to why 'Havana' didn't sell; it's a crudely fashioned, ineptly written half-hour which fails to sustain any interest."[21]

Abbott Mysteries

Bernard L. Schubert planned a new television series in 1956 based on the *Abbott Mysteries* series of books by Frances Cane. The characters of Pat Abbott and Jean Holly were a male/female detective team that first appeared in the 1941 novel, *The Turquoise Shop*, and then got married by the third book in the series, *The Yellow Violet*. Their adventures took them all over the globe.

When Schubert's plans for the series fell through, Desilu considered producing a pilot in 1957 with the concept similar to that of *The Thin Man*. However, this Desilu project never resulted in a pilot.

Private Eyeful

This spring 1958 pilot starred Marilyn Maxwell as private detective, Pat Barkley, in a hybrid comedy/crime series. Her co-star was Ron Randell as Lt. John Adams. Created by Eddie Buzzell, the planned series was first considered by Screen Gems. Based on the novels and short stories by detective writer, Henry Kane, Desilu produced the pilot in conjunction with Edward Buzzell Productions.

The pilot's story line had Pat Barkley visiting her friend Mama Satti (Lili Valento) who is concerned that her son Vittorio (Mike Connors), a carpenter, all of a sudden has a lot of cash. While Pat is questioning Vittorio about the money, he is shot and killed and a briefcase he had containing $100,000 is stolen. Pat contacts Lt. Adams and Sgt. Brad Williams (Frederick Ford) to report the murder and then goes to see Vittorio's former girlfriend Lola (Jean Allison) and informs her of the murder. Next Pat and Sgt. Williams visit Vittorio's current girlfriend, Rose Raven (Patricia Donahue). Pat and the police think that a man named Whisper (Casey Adams), who works for Rose Raven, killed Vittorio but, when questioned, he doesn't admit to the murder.

Later, a friend of Whisper's, Joe April (Claude Aikens) confides to Pat that Whisper is indeed the culprit. Whisper felt that he was entitled to the money in the briefcase. The cash was part of a life insurance payout that Whisper was after. Pat discovers that Vittorio's former girlfriend, Lola had changed her name in order to be the beneficiary of the policy. In the end, Lola agrees to give the life insurance money to Mama Satti.

Private Eyeful was a rare attempt at the time to showcase a female as a continuing character on a dramatic series.

Security Agent

Mort Briskin considered producing this 1958 pilot about special security agents in the missile and electronics fields. Martin Berkeley and Clark Reynolds wrote a treatment for the planned series, but nothing more was done on the project.

The treatment described the work of security agents protecting manufacturers of defense technology. Most of them are former FBI agents who try to prevent theft, subversion, espionage, and sabotage. The planned series would focus on Ramshead Electronics which develops electronic equipment for missiles, anti-attack warning devices, and anti-submarine elements.

The series would have centered on the work of Ed Fleming– a former FBI agent and judo expert who is multilingual. His first case involves an enemy agent who rises to a prominent position at Ramshead and has complete access to computers to alter calculations so that if a new missile experiment had been undertaken, the entire Southeast United States could have been destroyed.

Each story in the series would deal with some aspect of the world of science and space, the part men play in creating that world, the efforts of spies and traitors to undo that work, and the functioning of security agents to ferret them out.

Chick Bowdrie, Texas Ranger

In "No Place to Stop," a 1959 installment of Rory Calhoun's *The Texan* which was co-produced by Desilu, Calhoun's character, Bill Longley, becomes involved in the case of Noah Whipple, an ex-con on parole, who is working on his ranch when a gang of outlaws headed by old man Blackstone comes to town to drive Whipple from his property. Taking refuge in the town's hotel, Longley and Chick Bowdrie defend Whipple against the gang. Bowdrie, dressed all in black, had been captured by Indians when young and held by them for three years. The outlaws rope Whipple's daughter, who is returning to the hotel, which starts a gunfight killing one of the gang members. Longley and Bowdrie eventually take care of the rest of the gang with the help of an old lady at the hotel. Bowdrie then decides to become a Texas Ranger.

If *Chick Bowdrie, Texas Ranger* had become a series, the episodes would have been based on Louis L'Amour stories. L'Amour had written several short stories about the exploits of Chick Bowdrie which were collected in the novels, *Bowdrie* and *Bowdrie's Law*. Twenty-six episodes of the planned TV series were contemplated for syndication, but the only appearance of the Bowdrie character in a Desilu production was in *The Texan* episode.

Caballero

Starring Cesar Romero as Captain DaCosta, *Caballero* was another planned spin-off from *The Texan*. Bill Longley is in the southern part of the state when he is stopped by a group of Mexicans led by DaCosta. DaCosta thinks Bill is a Mr. Crawford, but when Longley says he is not, the group lets him go. DaCosta later meets Longley in San Tomas where an auction is being held for, among other items, boxes of rifles and ammunition. Both Longley and DaCosta compete in bidding on the guns but lose out to a woman named Katherine who wins the items for her guardian, Mr. Crawford (Whit Bessell). Crawford wants to sell the weapons to the Apaches for a profit.

After leaving Crawford's place, Longley and the Captain are followed by two of Crawford's henchman who want to kill the pair, but Longley and DaCosta take care of the men first. The two then cooperate to stop the sale of the rifles to the Indians in Mexico. DaCosta steals the wagon containing the guns and, with Longley and Katherine, drives it to a mountain cave. Katherine had decided to support the Texan and the Mexican. They are followed by Crawford's men. A shoot out occurs with DaCosta setting off an explosion in the cave. Crawford's men retreat leaving only Katherine's guardian. The weapons are covered under tons of stone. DaCosta shoots Crawford after the latter tries to kill him and Longley.

The back-door pilot aired April 13, 1959.

Homicide Squad (aka Homicide)

Beginning in fall 1959, Desilu sought to develop a one-hour series for ABC about a team of eight detectives in the Los Angeles Police Department. Actor Van Heflin was wanted for the role of captain of detectives. The production company planned to use a team of two big-named actors in every five out of thirteen episodes.

Ed Adamson and Harry Essex wrote the script for the pilot. By February 1961, the project was shelved because of lack of network interest. At the time, Desilu would not make a one-hour pilot without a network or co-production deal for financing.

Young Man with a Badge

Tommy Cook was to star in this 1959 police drama about a young cop who masquerades as a teenager to help break up and control youthful crime rings. Norman Retchin, a co-producer of *The Untouchables*, wrote the pilot script. Retchin's PEM Productions was to co-produce the series with Desilu.

In 1968, producers Aaron Spelling and Danny Thomas launched a similarly themed show called *The Mod Squad* about three youthful undercover cops.

Sheriff Squad

One of Desilu's most popular syndicated series, *Whirlybirds*, about two helicopter pilots, was distributed by CBS-TV Film Sales. *Whirlybirds* focused on the owners of a helicopter chartering company – Chuck Martin (Kenneth Tobey) and P.T. Moore (Craig Hill) who flew Bell helicopters. The series, which began in 1957 and ended in 1960, was originally supposed to air on the CBS network.

In a way, the idea of a show centered on helicopters grew out of a classic *I Love Lucy* episode, "Bon Voyage," where the Ricardo's and the Mertzes are about ready to sail to Europe but Lucy leaves the cruise ship to say one last "good-bye" to Little Ricky. The ship starts to sail away with Lucy's only chance to board the ship is to charter a helicopter to fly to the liner and hoist her down on its deck.

The final episode of *Whirlybirds* titled "Four Little Indians" was a backdoor, unsold pilot for a new syndicated series, *Sheriff Squad*, starring Richard Arlen as Lt. Chris Blake and John Agar as Sgt. Danny Flynn of the Los Angeles County Sheriff's Metropolitan Detail. A Deputy District Attorney is killed in a car crash which turns out not to have been an accident but a murder since the DA was shot before the crash. Next, a plane piloted by Danny Flynn and carrying Chris Blake and a Mr. Lane (James Bell) is having problems with a trim tab. It lands safely at the airport where the Whirlybird helicopters are located. Sabotage is suspected. The detectives inform Chuck Martin and P.T. Moore that Danny and Mr. Lane have both received letters stating "one down, four to go" and that the two helicopter pilots will also receive such letters.

The police suspect that Joe Kagan (Charles Aidman), an escaped prisoner charged with stealing $40,000 from Lane and Company, sent the letters because Kagan is seeking revenge on those whom he claims railroaded him into prison. The two police detectives visit Kagan's wife and realize that she is hiding her husband from the law. After being captured, Kagan denies robbing the company and killing the DA. Blake believes his story and asks P.T. and Chuck to act as bait to entice the DA's real killer into the open as police lie in wait to capture him. The killer flees after attempting to shoot P.T. and Chuck, but the Whirlybird pilots and the two detectives follow his vehicle in two separate copters.

The shooter goes to an industrial building. The two detectives engage in a shoot-out with the suspect who climbs a ladder in the building trying to escape. Danny topples the ladder, and the shooter falls to the ground. Danny and Chris discover that the shooter is Mr. Lane. The two detectives learn that Lane and his brother were behind the theft of $40,000 and the framing of Kagan for the crime. When Kagan escaped from prison, Lane wanted it to look like the ex-inmate was a crazed killer out for revenge and so killed the DA hoping that the police would then shoot Kagan on site and the real perpetrators of the theft would never be discovered.

The Violators

John Auer produced and Jack Jacobs wrote the script for this half-hour police drama in late 1960. The project concerned everyday people who become lawbreakers either by accident or intent.

Desilu had hoped to make a co-production deal on this project with singer Perry Como's company, Roncom, but no deal was reached. Apparently, no pilot was ever made. The project was shelved in February 1961.

Adventures of Jack London

Mort Briskin, in November 1960, secured the rights to author Jack London's works including his twenty-eight novels and all major stories and articles. London was born in 1876 and became an international celebrity and wealthy man from his writings. Best known for his novels *The Call of the Wild* and *White Fang*, he also wrote many short stories.

The planned Desilu series for syndication would have been set in the 1860s. The company was not sure if the series would be thirty or sixty minutes in length, but by February 1961, the project was shelved.

A previous attempt to base a TV series on the works of Jack London had been made in 1952. Titled *Jack London Theatre*, three episodes were filmed by Mutual Television Productions.

The Guardians

Desilu had hoped to have actor Jeff Chandler star in this 1961 thirty-minute project about the New York City Police Department and its relationship with teens who were not necessarily juvenile delinquents.

Originally, the concept for Chandler was to be featured in a *Casablanca*-type adventure series for Desilu. That idea was abandoned with Jerry Thorpe and David Goodman seeking to develop a show tentatively titled *Juvenile Officer* which then became *The Guardians*.

The Big Circuit

Jerry Thorpe and John Mantley tried to develop a series dealing with the behind-the-scenes activities of rodeos. For this 1961 effort, five continuing characters were planned – a widower horse contractor; his two sons - ages eighteen and thirteen; a rodeo clown; and the clown's daughter. NBC indicated some interest in the project, but by early 1962 the project was dead.

However, for the 1963-64 TV season Desilu was able to sell to ABC a similarly-themed series about a behind-the-scenes look at circus performers. Called *The Greatest Show on Earth* after the Cecil B. DeMille movie of the same title, the drama starred Jack Palance as circus-manager Johnny Slate who became involved in personal stories concerning his entertainers.

Locust 4-3931

Adrian Spies drafted an undated treatment for a Desilu drama about a police reporter who does undercover work for a city's new mayor. Joe Rogart calls the secret phone number, the planned series title, each day to report to the mayor information he uncovered concerning organized crime and corrupt police officers in the city. To keep their relationship a secret, the mayor and Rogart have created a public feud between them with the mayor portraying the reporter as a cocky wise guy.

Other characters in the projected series were Merman Proelich, Rogart's boyhood friend who is a police officer; Jerry Congleton, the corrupt political leader behind the mayor; and Rogart's father, a ne'er-do-well who lives with his son.

Spies outlined some possible story lines for the series. In one, Rogart is suspicious of a certain police detective. As a police reporter, he accompanies the detective on one of his cases. Gunfire breaks out. If the detective knows that Rogart suspects him of corruption, he could easily kill the reporter and claim it was an accident.

In another potential story for the show, an informer, with whom Rogart has worked, is arrested and then found dead in jail. Rogart must try to find out if the murder was the act of a fellow prisoner, the consequence of police brutality, or an attack by a corrupt officer.

A third story had Rogart investigating the behavior of one of the mayor's assistants who may be experiencing a mid-life crisis or may be having a guilty reaction from something more sinister.

Adrian Spies wrote several episodes of the *Westinghouse Desilu Playhouse* as well as episodes of *The Untouchables* and *Star Trek*.

Chapter 6: Desi's Somewhat Reality-Based Unsold Drama Pilots

One hallmark of several drama series and pilots made by Desilu under Desi Arnaz's leadership was basing them on the careers of real people or the workings of government and other types of real organizations. Often these projects, mainly Westerns and crime dramas, were done in semi-documentary style. But such undertakings were highly fictionalized and not historically accurate. Desilu's most successful such series was *The Untouchables*, discussed later in this book.

Before *The Untouchables*, the only Desilu series that made it to air that supposedly came from actual police cases was the *Walter Winchell Files* presenting stories from the reporter's work at the *New York Daily Mirror*. Despite the fact that, in 1953, Winchell, an ally of Senator Joseph McCarthy, had mentioned on his radio show that Lucille Ball had been a member of the Communist Party, a charge for which the comedienne had already been cleared by the House Un-American Activities Committee, Desi still decided to do business with the reporter.

The ABC series, which began in 1957, had Winchell involved in crime stories that he would later publish in the paper. The opener, "Country Boy," written by Adrian Spies, had two detectives, Harry Manzak (Jacques Aubuchon) and Angie De Matteo (William Kendes) along with Winchell investigating a burglary at a warehouse perpetrated by a man named "Country Boy" (Harry Dean Stanton) and two of his cohorts. Country Boy shoots the warehouse watchman and then flees in a hijacked cab along with his accomplices. The perpetrators stop the taxi and disappear into a building. Country Boy begins shooting at the police including the two detectives. Although his two accomplices are arrested, Country Boy escapes to another building and lets himself into one of the apartments with Manzak looking for him. Country Boy quickly puts on pajamas and slippers found in the apartment to pretend he is the tenant. The detective knocks on the apartment door. Suspicious that Country Boy is not the real tenant, Manzak pulls the plug on the lamp lighting the room. When Country Boy fires his gun, Harry shoots back killing the culprit.

The Winchell series lasted one season on ABC and then a few episodes were made for syndication before the reporter was hired to narrate episodes of *The Untouchables*.

The Texan, a Desilu Western, was a series featuring the fictionalized exploits of a real Texas gunfighter. Partnering with actor Rory Calhoun and producer Victor Orsatti, Desilu brought *The Texan*, the production company's only successful network Western, to television on September 29, 1958. In 1956, Calhoun and Orsatti had formed a company known as Rorvic Productions derived from the first names of the founders.

The Texan starred Calhoun as Bill Longley, a fast gun who roamed the Lone Star state helping people and thwarting evil doers. The show lasted for two seasons on CBS. Bill Longley was a real figure in the Old West. Born in Texas in 1851, he died twenty-seven years later. Far from thwarting evil doers, the real Longley was an evil doer – a psychopathic gunfighter who was responsible for multiple killings, mostly of people of color. He was executed by hanging on October 11, 1878.

Tales of Allan Pinkerton (aka The Pinkerton Story)

One of the first crime dramas that Desilu attempted was based on the files of Allan Pinkerton who founded the Pinkerton Detective Agency. William Spier was assigned to produce this 1955 pilot planned for ABC with scripts supervised by James D. Horan who had written a book, *The Pinkerton Story*, about the detective agency.

The stories were to be drawn from Allan Pinkerton's twenty volumes of his personal experiences from the Civil War to the beginning of the twentieth century. However, Pinkerton's estate refused to give Desilu permission to use the stories for the planned series.

Father Duffy of Hell's Kitchen

Made in early 1956 in association with producers Sam Bischoff and Dave Diamond, this pilot, written by Steve Fisher, featured Father Duffy played by Lloyd Nolan helping rehabilitate down-on-their luck individuals as well as counseling parishioners with their personal problems. The real Father Duffy had served as pastor of Holy Cross Church in the Hell's Kitchen section of New York City.

The pilot involved Father Duffy meeting with Betty Mullins Winowski about a promise that she broke. Betty committed to staying a virgin until marriage, but, when she was a teenager, she slept with Gino Morelli, her ex-boyfriend who later went to prison. Gino has now been released from incarceration. Betty worries that her current husband Ed will leave her after he finds out about her relationship with Gino.

Father Duffy meets with Ed who attests to his love for his wife. When the Father returns to his church, coincidentally, Gino Morelli is waiting for him. He says that he wants to be reunited with Betty. Gino, who is carrying a gun, leaves the Father telling him to inform Betty that the two need to meet at a private place or else there will be dire consequences.

Betty decides to see her ex-boyfriend. She reveals that she is married and that she and her husband have a young son, but Gino ignores her. He goes through her wallet to find out where she lives. Betty tries to warn her husband that Gino is on his way to confront him. But Gino arrives before Ed and the child can flee. He takes Ed and his son hostage at gun point wanting to exchange them for Betty. Betty, Duffy, and the police arrive at the Winowski residence with the Father volunteering to become Gino's hostage if he releases Ed and Ed Jr. Duffy climbs the stairs and enters the house. Gino, desperate, threatens to kill everyone. Duffy asks Gino to kill him first. The Father claims that Gino is trying to fill a void in his life from a decade of adolescence. Father Duffy remarks that God is who is really missing in Gino's life and because of this, Gino has been driven to his rash behavior. Gino pretends not to be phased, trying to toughen himself to murder Duffy – but cannot. Using the opportunity, Duffy takes the gun from Gino, and Ed tackles him to the ground.

Upon presenting the pilot to potential sponsors, one advertising agency wanted the character to be changed to a social worker instead of a priest to permit the main character to fall in love.

In response, Lloyd Nolan stated "They said 'Let's take his collar off and make him a settlement worker.' This doesn't strike any spark with me. I think 39 weeks of being a Mr. Do-Good can be pretty dull, and you wind up with egg on your face. It's not utilizing my talents. With this new concept, I fail to see any attraction or challenge."[22]

Desilu commissioned a new script by Jay Ingram called "Danny Violin" and thought of hiring Karl Malden for *Duffy of Hell's Kitchen*. Ultimately the production company decided against this move saying there are ample other sponsors interested in the project. However, *Duffy* never became a series.

Cowboy Detective

Martin Leeds thought about basing a series on the exploits of Charley Siringo, who, among other exploits in the nineteenth century, had been a Pinkerton detective. He chronicled his work as a detective in a 1912 book, *A Cowboy Detective: A True Story of Twenty-Two Years with a World-Famous Detective Agency*. Because the Pinkerton Agency would not permit him to use its name in the book, he referred to his employer as the "Dickenson" Agency. His book described all the investigations in which he was involved, such as a train robbery of the Denver and Rio Grande Railroad, the deaths of two wealthy mine owners blown up with dynamite, and the robbery of the Treadwill Gold Mill in Alaska.

The series was considered in late 1956. By February 1957, the idea was rejected.

The Flying Fish

In September 1957, Desilu sought to base a series on the work of detectives employed by the British Overseas Airways. TV actress Louise Paget was to produce the series based on case histories to be provided by Donald Fish, chief security officer of British Overseas Airways and formerly with Scotland Yard. However, by January 1958, the project was canceled.

John Wesley Hardin Family Project

In mid-1958, Desi Arnaz planned a one-hour Western based on stories about the John Wesley Hardin family of Texas. Desilu considered using six different stars for the projected series: three each would star on their own episodes, three each would star alongside one of the other stars, and three episodes would use all six stars. Actors considered for the series were Robert Mitchum, Van Heflin, and Van Johnson along with June Allyson, Joan Crawford, and either Barbara Stanwyck or Anne Baxter.

John Wesley Hardin, born in Texas in 1853, whose father was a Methodist minister, hence Hardin's first and middle names, was another real-life gunfighter, similar to Bill Longley of *The Texan*. Hardin killed his first victim, a former slave, when he was only fifteen. His life basically became a series of gambling, drinking, fights, and killings. Hardin married his first wife, Jane Bowen, in 1872 and was often participating with his relatives in cattle drives and gunfights. Related by marriage to a family named "Taylor," he became involved in a feud between that family and the Sutton family resulting in Hardin and his older brother together with members of the Taylor family assassinating the head of the Sutton clan.

Among his many murder victims was Deputy Sheriff Charles Webb whom he murdered in 1873. He was eventually convicted of that murder and sentenced to twenty-five years in state prison. Released from prison after fifteen years with time off for good behavior, Hardin, who had studied law while incarcerated, passed the bar examination and set up a law practice in Gonzales, Texas. He also wrote his autobiography. After his first wife died, John Wesley married fifteen-year-old Callie Lewis, but she soon left him. On August 15, 1895, Hardin was killed by a man with whom he had been arguing.

It is not clear exactly what facets of Hardin's life would have been portrayed in the planned series or which of his many relatives would have been featured. Perhaps the series would have focused on Hardin's law career after prison despite the fact that he soon let his practice slide and returned to his old ways. No pilot for the series was ever made.

Privateer

Starring Fernando Lamas as real-life pirate and smuggler, Jean Lafitte, this 1959 attempt was a swashbuckling adventure set in 1800's New Orleans. Mort Briskin produced the pilot based on a script by Frank Moss.

According to *Variety*, as early as 1956, Briskin considered making this pilot, then titled, *Adventures of Jean Lafitte*, with actor Jacques Bergerac in the lead role.[23] But negotiations with the actor couldn't be finalized.

Intelligence Squad

This potential series, intended for syndication, was another effort developed by Mort Briskin beginning in 1958. It was based on the work of the Intelligence Squad of the Los Angeles Police Department. The series would focus on special police investigators working on secret undercover operations.

Reportedly, the material for the planned series was initially secured for Briskin's *Grand Jury* show - a Desilu production syndicated by NTA. *Grand Jury* involved cases investigated by Harry Driscoll (Lyle Bettger) and John Kennedy (Harold J. Stone). The two grand jury investigators looked into crimes such as protection rackets, drug syndicates, bribery, and insurance scams. The series lasted for two seasons from 1958 to 1960.

There was discussion at Desilu about whether *Intelligence Squad* would be a thirty or sixty-minute series. Because, at the time, the company could not afford to finance one-hour shows without network involvement or a co-production deal, the project was canceled in 1961.

Dallas

In May 1959, Desilu made a one-hour pilot for a Western starring John Bromfield. The actor played a former gunfighter who is chosen as the marshal by a group of gamblers who run the city of Dallas, Texas. The gamblers believe they can control the new marshal, but he and his partner, Doc Andrews, won't be corrupted.

The proposed series was based on actual characters who lived in Dallas around 1870 when the population of the city was 18,000.

When the initial pilot wasn't picked up as a series, Desilu remade it turning it into a half-hour Western. But that version also failed to become a series.

John Bromfield star of Sheriff of Cochise *and* U. S. Marshal *– both modern-day Westerns.*

Bromfield had previously starred in *Sheriff of Cochise*, the most popular syndicated series that came out of the Desilu – NTA association. He played Frank Morgan, the head lawman of Cochise County, Arizona. The show was a contemporary Western replacing horses with automobiles. It began in 1956 lasting until 1958 when its title changed to *U.S. Marshal*, and the John Bromfield character became the marshal for the entire state of Arizona. Reportedly, the new role for Bromfield covering all of Arizona allowed expanded story ideas. *U.S. Marshal* lasted until 1960.

Apparently, the half-hour version of the *Dallas* pilot aired as an episode of *U.S. Marshal* titled "Grandfather." Since *U.S. Marshal* was set in the present and *Dallas* in the 1870's, the *Marshal* episode involved a flashback with an author researching a book about Western lawmen who asks Frank Morgan to relate tales about his grandfather's career as a peace officer.

Secret Service Agent

Quinn Martin was set to produce this hour-length pilot for ABC that was first discussed in November 1959. The possible series would be based on the arm of the federal government in charge of Presidential security and preventing counterfeiting. Production was set for mid-January 1960, but a pilot was never made.

Martin left Desilu in March 1960 to create his own production company which subsequently made series like *The Fugitive*, *The FBI*, *Cannon*, and *Barnaby Jones*.

Ten Top Wanted Men

Martin Leeds pursued this December 1959 project – a one-hour drama about the most wanted criminals in the United States. Presumably, the proposed series would have been based on the FBI's list of wanted fugitives, but details surrounding the project are virtually non-existent.

Although it may not be directly related, the Desilu-produced police drama, *U. S. Marshal*, aired an episode in November 1959 titled, "One of the Ten Most Wanted Men." It dealt with the "Houdini of hoodlums" who tries a daring escape with four killers gunning for him and Marshal Frank Morgan on his trail.

Ten Top Wanted Men was tied to ABC. By May 1960, the concept for the series had been abandoned.

The Man from Telegraph Hill

Dick and Mary Sale created this adventure series focusing on Herb Caen, a real-life journalist for the *San Francisco Chronicle*. The planned one-hour series was initially to be developed by Screen Gems before Desilu expressed interest. Dan Dailey was set for the lead in late 1960, but by March 1961, Desilu postponed the project.

The pilot script, written by Dick Sale and titled "Don't Call It Frisco," outlined several characters in addition to Caen who would appear in the series: Fran Nelson, Caen's executive secretary; Pamela Nelson, Fran's daughter; Priscilla Fong, Caen's secretary; Lee Fong, her father; Cassandra Bellama, another of Caen's secretaries; and Willy "Dismal" Winkie, Caen's leg man who collected material for the columnist.

The story line had Caen going to Alcatraz, accompanied by two FBI agents, to speak with a convicted bank robber who is about to die. Leo Mannix is in prison for masterminding a bank robbery that resulted in the deaths of three tellers and a police officer. The $400,000 from the robbery has never been recovered, and Mannix wants to tell Caen where the money is so Mannix's wife can collect the $25,000 reward for finding the loot. Mannix's hospital room is wired so the FBI agents can monitor Caen's discussion with the inmate. However, the columnist passes a note to Mannix notifying him to write down the location of the stolen money.

When the agents think that Caen has failed to get the information from Mannix, they rush to the room, but Mannix passes away. Caen advises the agents to do an autopsy on Mannix because he thinks the inmate was poisoned. Because the FBI agents suspect that Mannix gave the newspaper reporter the location of the money, one of them shadows Caen. The reporter phones Priscilla telling her to have her father go to the location Mannix gave him and dig up the loot hidden in two aluminum suitcases.

A woman posing as Mannix's wife Lily finds the columnist and takes him to her apartment where he is knocked unconscious. Dr. Mark Carter, the prison doctor who was treating Mannix, is there along with two ambulance attendants. They put Caen in an ambulance and pick up Dan Whistler, a local gangster. Carter informs Whistler that Caen knows where the $400,000 is, and then the doctor injects Caen with truth serum. After the columnist divulges the location, the group goes to find the money. While Carter, Whistler, and the others are out of the ambulance looking for the loot, Caen is able to escape. Whistler and his men find an empty hole where the money had been. Prissy and Dismal find Caen in the road and also discover the body of Dr. Carter whom Whistler had one of his henchmen kill. Later, from Dismal, Whistler obtains information on where the stolen cash is and heads there to find Prissy, her father, Caen, and the FBI.

Richard Sale outlined other possible stories for the proposed series based on Herb Caen's columns about the denizens of San Francisco. One is about a gambler who goes to Las Vegas to make money, but he loves San Francisco so much he comes back even if the cops are after him. Another story involves the owner of a shop which sells herbs and fragrant ointments. When window washers clean the windows in the building next door, they feel sorry for the man whose shop windows are very dirty. They wash his windows for free. He thanks them but then is in trouble because his shop is a front for a business that needs dingy windows.

O.C.D. (Official Crime Division)

In June 1961, Desi Arnaz greenlighted this potential series about the Official Crime Division of the Chicago Police Department. It was planned as a sixty-minute series, but no writer or producer was ever assigned to the project, and no actors hired.

No Man Walks Alone

In August 1961, Mort Briskin proposed a one-hour drama set in Chicago in 1900. It would have focused on a former preacher who now functions as a volunteer public defender in criminal cases involving injustice. The ex-minister would be partnered with a young, crusading attorney in the show.

As with several other Desilu series based on real people or organizations, this proposed series would have had a semi-documentary flavor and would be based on actual cases taken from the files of the John Howard Association, a civic reform group. No pilot appears to have been made. The project was canceled in 1962.

Chapter 7: Desilu's Unsold Anthology Pilots

Anthologies were a mainstay of prime-time television in the 1950s and 1960s. The two anthologies that Desilu launched were *Official Detective* in syndication and *The Westinghouse-Desilu Playhouse* on CBS. The latter anthology is discussed in the next chapter.

Official Detective was an anthology featuring different crime stories each week based on the files of *Official Detective* magazine. Everett Sloane hosted the series which ran from 1957 to 1958. Stories included ones involving a psychopath terrorizing a city, the search for thieves who always hold a party at the scene of their robberies, and armored car heists.

Desilu endeavored to make other such series as outlined below but to no avail.

Anthology of Suspense

Also, titled *Desilu Mystery Theater*, this series attempt, developed by William Spier, was Desilu's initial venture into the anthology genre.

The 1956 pilot for the planned series, titled "The Silver Frame," starred Scott Brady. It involved a former inmate named Steve Gates, convicted of manslaughter, who feels he was framed for the crime and wants revenge on the District Attorney who convicted him based on circumstantial evidence. After he is released from prison, a newspaper reporter, Malvin Lester, approaches Gates about getting revenge on the District Attorney. Lester proposes that Gates stage the murder of a woman and leave evidence at the scene that Gates is the culprit. After Gates is arrested, Lester's paper will run a story about the police picking on ex-cons. Three days after the supposed murder when the so-called victim re-appears, the paper will do an article about the DA always relying on circumstantial evidence in this case and all other cases. Steve agrees to the plan with the promise of $500 in return. Later, a man named Milo delivers the $500 to Steve's hotel room from the publisher of the paper, Mr. Rosson. Lester phones Gates and advises where to meet the female victim.

Gates goes to the Malibu beach house where he encounters Silver Foxe (Joy Page). The murder is staged with Foxe being driven away from the house by Milo but not before giving Gates a recording of her voice to play to make it sound to the neighbors like he is killing her. A neighbor hears the commotion, sees Steve in the driveway of the house, and phones the police who are waiting, along with the DA, when he arrives back at his hotel room. The police not only accuse Steve of the murder but say they found the body of the dead woman. Steve attempts to explain the plan but is informed that Malvin Lester is dead. He asks the police to take him to the beach house to reenact the supposed murder. While there, he is able to escape through an open window and runs into Milo who says he will take him to see Rosson. Silver Foxe is at Rosson's place and claims that Milo is her brother. She remarks that Rosson, who is very fond of her, took out a $300,000 insurance policy on her life with Milo as beneficiary. Even though Rosson contends that the original plan described by Malvin Lester was supposed to take place, Foxe conspired with Milo to modify the plan to get the insurance money. Milo killed Lester as well as a woman whose burnt body the police found thinking she was Foxe. Silver and Milo were then to flee out of the country with the money.

When Gates wants to turn Milo into the police, Milo tries to shoot him. Silver fires at Milo, killing him and relates that he was not really her brother. She also wants to kill Rosson so that she and Steve can run away together. Steve knocks her unconscious and has Rosson explain the entire story to the police.

The Orson Welles Show

The esteemed actor/writer/producer, Orson Welles, made his situation comedy debut on a 1956 episode of *I Love Lucy* playing himself with Lucy becoming his assistant in his magic act.

One consequence of appearing on the comedy was that Desilu commissioned Welles to do a pilot for his own anthology series to be called *The Orson Welles Show*. For the black and white show that he did for Desilu, Welles, the master storyteller, wrote, directed, produced, and served as the on-camera host and narrator. Sometimes, he even mouthed the characters' words while still photos of them appeared giving the pilot the feel of a documentary. According to Desi Arnaz, he was the one who suggested to Welles that he wanted a different type of setting for the host of an anthology series. Instead of the host being on the same set each week to introduce an episode, he wanted Welles to appear as though he were "... in front of the television set in the viewer's living room, telling them what is happening or about to happen..."[24]

The 1956 pilot titled, "The Fountain of Youth," set in the 1920's, was based on a short story by John Collier called "Youth from Vienna." The stars were Dan Tobin as Dr. Humphrey Baxter, an endocrinologist involved in developing an experimental youth serum, Joi Lansing, the beautiful blonde actress Caroline Coates, and Rick Jason, handsome tennis pro Alan Brodie. As Welles explains at the outset, "eternal triangle plus eternal youth equals a wacky little romance."

The story begins with Baxter attending a play starring twenty-three year-old Caroline Coates. He meets and falls in love with her, but, before they marry, he has to return to Vienna to resume his experiments with renowned Dr. Vingleberg in developing a serum that stops the aging process. After three years abroad, he returns and learns that Caroline has fallen in love with someone else, a tennis star named Alan Brodie whom she wants to marry.

Humphrey contacts a magazine reporter to inform him that he has isolated a glandular secretion that controls aging. Upon returning from her honeymoon with Brodie, Caroline and her new husband visit Baxter and want him to stop their aging. He explains that the anti-aging formula is not yet readily available. He says that he does have one sample that he could give them as a wedding gift but that they cannot each simply take half. For it to work, a full dose must be administered. The couple goes home and discusses who should take the serum. Each wants the other to take it. Both being concerned about growing older, Brodie finally swallows the dose and fills the empty bottle with a liquid that tastes bitter. Not knowing this, Caroline later consumes the contents of the bottle and refills it with water and quinine.

After some time, Caroline leaves her husband and confesses to Humphrey that she took the dose and no longer loves Brodie. When she says that the dose tasted bitter, Baxter responds that he just put salt in some water to fool the couple into thinking he had found the fountain of youth.

At the end of the story, Welles says that next week's episode titled "Green Thoughts" would be about a man-eating tiger orchid – a spook story with a seasoning of giggles. While that episode description may have sounded like some Wellesian humor, Mr. Welles did indeed want to film another short story by John Collier about a unique orchid that a Mr. Mannering receives. Initially, the blossoms on the orchid resemble flies' heads. But then strange happenings occur in the Mannering house when first, his cousin's cat disappears, and subsequently the cousin herself is nowhere to be found. The orchid flourishes with blossoms that unmistakably resemble the cat and the cousin. Readers can probably guess who disappears next. Dann Cahn, who edited "The Fountain of Youth," recalled Welles talking about this next episode saying "I got it all in my head, Danny. I'm going to take that short story and that'll be our second show."[25]

Originally, Welles sought to do a one-hour anthology series, but CBS demanded a thirty-minute show. Martin Leeds had a luncheon date with Welles to tell him what the network wanted. Welles questioned why not an hour series. Leeds responded. "Because an hour is not commercial – you can't sell it in syndication."[26] Welles then bellowed for all to hear, "How dare you talk to me about crass commercialism!"[27]

The sixty-minute anthology proposal may have been *Theater on Film*, a planned drama presenting top stage plays which would have included a live studio audience. Arnaz and Welles believed that having people sitting in front of the stage would give the performers a different "feel" and this would transmit itself to the TV viewing audience. The first play was to be *Valpone* scheduled to be filmed by May 15, 1956. The anthology would air once a month. While Orson would appear in about one out of four shows, *The Billboard* speculated that Desi and Lucy would star in some of the other plays.[28]

There was also a compromise proposal to do thirty-minute episodes and then, once every two months, a one-hour show. The half-hour shows were to demonstrate Welles' versatility by having him do readings on one installment, magic tricks on another, and dramatic portrayals in still others.

Other than "The Fountain of Youth" pilot, nothing came of these proposals.

Woman in the Case

This proposed anthology had a lengthy history of being shopped around to various production companies including Desilu.

George Burns' McCadden Productions announced in summer 1957 that it was working with June Havoc and William Spier on a vehicle starring the actress. Spier and Havoc were to own a 25% share of the project, and Havoc was to star in and host several of the episodes on a rotating basis with other female stars. Other actresses mentioned as possibilities for hostess duties included Ida Lupino, Anne Baxter, Teresa Wright, Bette Davis, and Lilli Palmer.

Woman in the Case would deal mostly with women involved some way in criminal cases. In his proposal, Spier outlined a few story lines. One centered on Jane Stanton, a librarian at the Glendale Public Library, who receives a book returned by a woman with two pages missing. The woman disavows being the culprit who tore out the pages complaining that because of the missing pages she was deprived of a hot love scene. Jane finds strange razor cuts on the pages on each side of those missing from the book. She then compares the vandalized copy of the book with one from which no pages have been removed. She discovers that certain words have been cut out by the razor blade. Jane makes a list of the words and determines that, when placed in the right order, the words are part of a ransom note.

Another story line concerned an out-of-work actress named Pat Dodger who is a member of the Office of Special Services and Investigation, an undercover unit of the police department. Pat was likely to turn up anywhere there was a murder, missing person, or a narcotics ring, and she would play a variety of undercover roles such as a lady cellist or a cigarette girl.

Negotiations between Burns' company and the Spier's never resulted in McCadden producing a pilot of *Woman in the Case*.

The series idea was then shopped to Desilu with the idea that the anthology would feature stories based on Agatha Christie mysteries. By November 1957, Desi Arnaz envisioned a series consisting of crime stories and strong dramas with four actresses starring on a rotating basis – two younger actresses and two older ones. Piper Laurie and Phyllis Thaxter were considered for the former and Maureen O'Hara and Claire Trevor (or perhaps Bette Davis) for the latter. The Desilu concept for the series was created by Quinn Martin who indicated the format for the planned show would start with the female host introducing herself and then a brief scene with no dialogue would appear for a few seconds. Next the main title credits would be displayed fading into the first commercial. The first act would either be a continuation of the opening action or a scene that would normally follow it dramatically. At the end of the episode, the host of the subsequent week's story would have a short tag to evoke interest for the next show. Summing up the concept, Martin indicated, "We plan for the 'Woman in the Case' to cover every crime that a woman can commit, and we hope to advance a little – if only very little – within our series, a more comprehensive insight into one of the most fascinating things in the world – the female mind."[29]

The pilot for the anthology, titled "The Ninth Commandment," was written by David Harmon based on a story by Quinn Martin. Mary Smith, a seamstress at a clothing factory who lives in a small apartment with her roommate Sandra, witnesses a man rushing past her on the stairs of her apartment building and then discovers the dead body of another tenant. Interrogated by the police and photographed by reporters, the next day at work her boss offers Mary a promotion to receptionist having liked the fact that she mentioned the name of the company where she works in her interviews with the press. She receives a raise and new wardrobe with reporters continuing to put her in the limelight about what she witnessed. Mary didn't really get a good look at the man who rushed past her and so can't positively identify the murderer from a police line-up. However, at the urging of the District Attorney, she takes another look at the suspects in the line-up and identifies one of them as the culprit. Liking that she is the star witness at the criminal trial, she positively identifies the defendant as the murderer, and he is convicted. After the man goes to prison, his defense attorney attempts to persuade Mary to change her testimony. She says she would only do this if the attorney can find the man wo really committed the crime. Seven months after the end of the trial, the real murderer is found. Next day at work, Mary is demoted back to her old job as a seamstress and goes back to her previous life style out of the limelight.

By April 1958, Desilu abandoned the project.

Come October 1958, William Dozier at CBS became interested in the project with Maureen O'Hara hosting and starring in thirteen of the projected thirty-nine episodes. Planned for the 1959-60 season, O'Hara starred with Tony Randall in the pilot for the show called "Open Windows," written by J.P. Miller and directed by Mitchell Leisen.

Based on the initial pilot script, apparently the concept of the proposed O'Hara series differed dramatically from the original book and the other proposed story lines. The script focused on Kate (O'Hara) and Bill Craig (Randall) who are in the process of divorcing. Kate, thirty-two, is packing to leave her apartment in an upper-middle class section of New York City when she sees her ex-husband Bill, a thirty-five-year-old corporate lawyer, approaching the building. She had hoped to vacate the premises before he arrived. Bill is surprised that Kate is still there and is not taking all of her possessions with her, in particular the clothes Bill had bought for her which he thought she wanted. Kate confesses that she never really liked the items Bill purchased and that she resented Bill for treating her like a possession. Bill divulges that he just quit his job with the family law firm and that he always wanted to be a horticulturist but deferred that career when he met Kate in order to keep her in the style to which she had become accustomed. Bill then asks Kate to give their marriage a second chance, but Kate leaves. From the open apartment window, Bill yells down to her in the street about meeting some night. Kate relents and replies "yes."

Seemingly, the Maureen O'Hara version of *The Woman in the Case* would have been less crime drama and more romantic dramedy which is no doubt why CBS, when trying to find sponsors for the proposed series, changed its title to *Men & Women*.

In 1960, Paul Monash at MGM attempted to make a pilot deal with NBC for the series, but the network rejected this project in 1961 because of excessive costs.

Famous Artists Anthologies

Desi Arnaz concluded a deal in early 1958 with Sam Jaffe of Famous Artists Associates, a talent agency, to produce a thirty-minute anthology starring actors and actresses and using directors and producers represented by the agency. The deal would also utilize staff from Famous Artists literary department.

One concept for the anthology offered by writer William Spier was to base each story on some written document. Tentatively to be called *The Moving Finger*, as Spier indicated in a letter to Jaffe, "Any desired kind of story with urgency will fit into this scheme... A doctor writes out a prescription for a patient... A wife writes a note to her husband saying she is leaving him.... A business executive writes a memo... A judge jots down a note of some detail pertaining to a trial in progress...."30

While it is not known if that concept for the series was ever developed, Desi Arnaz did make a pitch to have Desilu produce a Famous Artists anthology as a replacement for Revue making the installments of *General Electric Theatre*. Desi would have probably become the executive producer of the General Electric anthology with Ronald Reagan continuing to host the series. Another alternative would have been to replace Reagan with actor George Murphy. However, by May 1958, negotiations had collapsed.

In December 1960, about two and a half years after the initial deal with Famous Artists didn't get off the ground, Desi and the talent agency contemplated another initiative for a horror/adventure-type series. The planned series, *Fright*, would feature artist Salvador Dali as host and narrator with the show using his designs and drawings. But, as with the prior initiative, this one also never went anywhere.

Actor Hugh O'Brien, whose *Life and Legend of Wyatt Earp* series filmed at Desilu Studios, was interested in producing the Dali series.

The Arlene Dahl Show

While her then-husband, Fernando Lamas, was working on the Desilu pilot, *The Privateer*, his wife, Arlene Dahl, was involved with the production company in starring in an anthology pilot written by Adrian Spies. Similar to *The Lorretta Young Show*, the Dahl show planned to have the actress introducing each episode as well as starring in some.

The pilot script begins with Ms. Dahl standing at the top of a grand stairway in a beautiful house with the following description, "Arlene Dahl is there, magnificently-dressed, radiant, smiling down at us with the gracious, quiet smile of (a) woman secure in her own beauty."31

Dahl plays a young woman named Connie who works as a stenographer at the Blue Isles Hotel. Her parents are visiting for the weekend. They feel that their daughter has let them down by divorcing her husband of five years. After her parents leave, Leo Benedict, age fifty-seven, a guest at the establishment, asks Connie to transcribe some letters and have dinner with him. While attempting to dictate correspondence with little success, Benedict confesses that the only reason he asked for her stenographic services was to invite her to dinner. Despite this revelation, Connie still wants to have dinner. Over a week, their relationship develops even though he is more than twice her age. The following weekend, when her parents visit again, she introduces Leo to them. Her mother makes a veiled remark about Benedict's age which upsets him. Later, he asks Connie to marry him. She has to think about it but finally accepts his proposal.

Dahl appears again as herself at the end noting that the couple "lived happily ever after."

For Men Only

In December 1959, Desilu started development of an anthology targeted to male viewers. Lee J. Cobb was to host the program and occasionally star in episodes dealing with high-octane, blood and guts adventure stories.

A ten-minute presentation film was made in April 1960 that seemed to focus more on humor than high adventure. ABC considered picking up the project, but by May 1960 the project was dead.

Villa Marina

Before Aaron Spelling produced semi-anthologies like *Love Boat* and *Hotel* with a continuing supporting cast of characters, Desilu's Mort Briskin created this anthology which would take place at the plush Villa Marina resort in Newport Beach, California. In addition to villas, apartments, a nightclub and a dining room, the resort had a marina that accommodated over 300 boats.

The concept of the proposed series was to focus on the guests at the resort and feature mystery, romance, drama, and comedy stories. Lex Barker was considered for the role of Chip Casey, the owner-operator of the Villa Marina with Hoagy Carmichael playing Ralph "Easy" Simons, the marina's piano player.

The pilot script, written by Don Martin, was a murder-mystery to be made in early 1959. It appears that Briskin resurrected this idea in 1966 when he created the pilot for Desi Arnaz Productions titled *Land's End*. See Chapter 20 for more information.

Anatomy of...

In 1961, Desilu thought about producing an anthology created by Ben Brady. *Anatomy of...* would be a "point of view" concept dealing with the examination and study of people and events like the anatomy of a murder.

Brady wrote a story for an episode titled "Anatomy of a Confession" about the consequences to a District Attorney when he learns that he may have convicted the wrong man for murder. DA Edward Wylie is called to the hospital to interview a dying patient, Arthur Chapin, who confesses that he was responsible for a robbery and murder for which another man had been sentenced to death and died in the electric chair. Chapin instructs Wylie on where he hid the gun and cash from the crime. After performing a ballistics test on the gun, the weapon is found to indeed have been the one used in the killing. George Claremont, Wylie's chief political backer, is told of the results before Wylie is.

Wylie is advised not to inform the press of the new confession until an investigation is performed to determine if it is a political frame-up since Wylie aspires to higher office. When there is no evidence that his political enemies are behind the confession, Wylie schedules a press conference, but before he meets the press, he is told that the transcript of Chapin's confession is missing and that his assistant who witnessed the confession along with him has gone on vacation. His political backers want him to keep the confession a secret so he doesn't ruin his political career. Wylie returns to the hospital to interview Chapin again to make sure he is telling the truth. When Chapin stands by his confession, Wylie finally decides to give the full story to the newspapers.

While the story was written by Ben Brady, the teleplay, which appears to have never been produced, was done by John McGreevey.

Victor Borge Comedy Theatre

In white tie and tails, Victor Borge hosted this anthology of comedy sketches described as "comedy diversification" – all types of comedy under one roof. The pilot, made in early 1962, presented three playlets:

"Suzuki Beane" – a story told by a little girl named Suzuki (Katie Sweet) who lives in Greenwich Village with her parents – a poet father and a sculptor mother. Still photos were used primarily in relating the tale about her life at school and her adventures with her friend Henry (Jimmy Garrett, later Lucy's son on *The Lucy Show*).

"Transportation Story" – written by Madelyn Martin and Bob Carroll, Jr. and directed by Desi Arnaz. Lucille Ball and Gale Gordon starred in this story about Lucy taking her first flight to Europe. Having never flown before, she has trouble buckling her seat belt, uses the chewing gum offered by the flight attendant to plug her ears, gets drunk on champagne, and mistakenly blows up her life jacket causing the other passengers to think the plane is crashing into the ocean.

The playlet was later adapted for an October 17, 1966 episode of *The Lucy Show*, "Lucy Flies to London," where Lucy Carmichael wins a free trip to London and is on the same plane from Los Angeles to New York as Mr. Mooney. That episode aired a week before "Lucy in London," a sixty-minute special that featured Lucy touring England's capital city.

"The Sound and the Fidelity" – A wife (Sarah Marshall) is planning an elegant cocktail hour for her husband (Tom Ewell) which is disrupted by the new neighbors playing a sound effects record. The couple thinks the house is being bombarded until they realize from where the sound is coming. When the neighbors don't comply with a request to reduce the noise, the husband buys his own sound effects recording of volcano eruptions.

ABC expressed some interest in this potential series but then backed off. CBS subsequently sought to make a deal for the project. In February 1962, Desilu screened the pilot before an audience to add laughter but didn't receive much of a response. As might be expected, the Lucy segment received the most laughs. The Tom Ewell playlet received almost none. This test did not stimulate much enthusiasm at CBS. The pilot never became a series.

The United States Immigration Story

In an October 25, 1962 story in *Variety* about Desilu's plans for pilots for the 1963-64 season, there is mention that Arnaz was contemplating an anthology about people who came to America and made good. While there are no further details about this project, a treatment for a potential series under the general title, *The United States Immigration Story*, is among the William Spier/June Havoc Papers at the Wisconsin Historical Society.

The undated treatment lays out some tentative format ideas and titles:

1. *Ellis Island* would be a possible title for a show focusing on New York City and the new citizens from Europe arriving through that port of entry in the shadow of the Statue of Liberty.
2. *Five Ports* or *Port of Entry* as a title would enlarge the concept of the series to show immigrants from all parts of the world. Each episode would concentrate on one of the ports of entry – New York City, New Orleans, Chicago, San Francisco, and Los Angeles.
3. Other titles considered included *The Citizen*, *Naturalized Citizen*, *Pursuit of Happiness*, *First Papers*, and *Brave New World*.

Regardless of the title, the proposed series would open and close in the offices of the U.S. Immigration and Naturalization Service as ICE was then called. A narrator would relate stories based on the files of that agency with the time period for each episode ranging from the early years in the settlement of the country to the present day.

One potential episode was outlined dealing with the Lewksowski family who immigrated in 1910. The head of the Polish family seeks to have his niece Anna come to the United States. Poppa fills out the immigration form the way he thinks it should be completed. He completes the form incorrectly meaning the information must be changed before Anna arrives by ship. Papa is worried that his niece will not be able to enter the country and also that he may lose his job since everyone knows a man from Immigration visited him. However, a young man from the steamship company goes to the authorities, fixes everything, and brings Anna to the Lewksowski home. Five years after her arrival, Anna applies for papers to become a U.S. citizen.

Evidently, no pilot resulted from Spier's treatment.

Chapter 8: Westinghouse-Desilu Playhouse Spin-offs

Desi Arnaz's most ambitious undertaking as head of Desilu was an anthology titled *Desilu Playhouse,* sponsored by Westinghouse. The idea for this anthology began as early as 1955 with Desi stating that he and Lucy wanted to broaden their scope of activity feeling that the trend on television was toward the hour-long series. As Arnaz later noted, "In early 1958 I prepared a presentation of the Desilu Playhouse, an hour weekly show which I would host. We didn't make a pilot, just a rundown on the type of stories we would do. Some of them would be dramas, some adventure and some mystery, all designed for family viewing, and a *Lucille Ball-Desi Arnaz Show* every third or fourth week of the series, intended for the 1958-1959 season."[32] He went on to remark, "I came back to California with the biggest contract ever negotiated for television. It called for 41 *Desilu Playhouses,* one *Lucy Special,* two *Desi Specials* and eight more *Lucy-Desi Comedy Hours* for the next two years."[33] At the time, the $12 million deal with Westinghouse was the biggest TV contract ever negotiated.

Arnaz indicated that the regular episodes of the anthology would not be designed as star vehicles but instead would emphasize dramatic values.[34]

To publicize the upcoming series to Westinghouse dealers, the cast of *I Love Lucy* filmed a thirty-minute infomercial. Lucy, Desi, Vivian Vance, and William Frawley appeared as themselves but really played their characters from the sitcom. The story line concerned Lucy wanting to buy all new Westinghouse appliances for her dressing room despite the fact that Desi asks her to postpone the purchase.

The show opens with Lucy as Vice President of Desilu scanning a catalog of Westinghouse products. She and her husband argue over the pronunciation of "Westinghouse" with Desi wanting to pronounce it as "Westingouse." Desi is taking Mr. Haydn (Ross Elliott), a representative of Westinghouse on a tour of Desilu. Vivian Vance and Bill Frawley drop by Desi's office and invite Lucy out to lunch. While Desi accompanies Haydn on a helicopter tour, Lucy plots with Viv and Bill about how to circumvent Desi's wishes.

While Viv and Bill distract Desi, Lucy dons various disguises to discuss her Westinghouse order with Haydn after the aerial tour of Desilu is over. First, she appears as a helicopter mechanic to talk with Haydn, and then as a set painter while Desi is showing Haydn the stage where "Bernadette," the premiere episode of *Desilu Playhouse* is being filmed. Lucy is dressed as a Mexican on the set of the first *Lucille Ball-Desi Arnaz Show* titled "Lucy Goes to Mexico" that will be sponsored by Westinghouse. Finally, in the property room at Desilu Studios where Bill and Viv show the miniature of King Kong used in the movie, Lucy, in a gorilla outfit, asks Haydn to deliver her purchase as quickly as possible. In the end, Desi visits Lucy's dressing room and finds it full of Westinghouse products with Lucy hiding in a clothes dryer.

Vance and Frawley as well as Lucy and Desi also played themselves on an episode of *Desilu Playhouse* called the "Desilu Revue." Lucy is planning a Christmas party for all the company's staff. Hedda Hopper appears wanting to write a column about the talented players Lucy has mentored as part of her Desilu Workshop.

Desi then flashes back to the live opening of the revue with Lucy's sixteen singers and dancers. Ms. Ball is very nervous about her students' debut and wants to give each of them notes concerning their upcoming performances. Desi advises Viv and Bill to keep Lucy from backstage because she is making the performers anxious. In Lucy Ricardo-style, she tries sneaking in to give the entertainers her notes. Most of the stars from the Desilu-produced and filmed television shows were in the audience for the revue including Spring Byington, Rory Calhoun, Ann Sothern, and Danny Thomas. Lucille Ball herself was listed as the producer of this December 25, 1959 episode.

Besides hosting most of the episodes of *Desilu Playhouse*, Desi Arnaz starred as a character other than himself on two installments. Airing October 30, 1959 and guest hosted by George Murphy, Desi portrayed Luis Martinez living with his family in an impoverished neighborhood in a city in Florida similar to Sarasota or Tampa. The episode by Adrian Spies was titled "So Tender, So Profane." Martinez is faced with a moral decision when his sister, Emelia (Barbara Luna) arrives for an extended stay with the family.

Luis Martinez works in a cigar factory and lives in the Spanish section of the Florida town with his wife Francesca (Adele Mara) and young daughter Antonia. He is displeased when his sister Emelia is planning to stay with his family because she is a prostitute known to the local police, in particular to a Detective Silvera (Pedro Armendariz) who had questioned Emelia awhile back about a male acquaintance of hers accused of a crime.

After Emelia arrives, Luis takes her and his family out for dinner where Silvera and his wife (Margo) are also eating. Silvera begins to stare at Emelia with an expression of lust on his face noticed by his wife. The detective comes to Martinez's table seeming very interested in Emelia, learns where she will be working, and says he often visits that neighborhood. A few days later, Luis discovers that the detective attempted to hook up with Emelia. She decides to leave town before Silvera comes to Luis' home to pick her up. Luis decides to confront the detective. He tells Silvera to leave Emelia alone and threatens to go to police headquarters and inform authorities what the detective has been doing.

Silvera leaves but decides to force a drug addict that he knows into implicating Luis in a recent robbery at the cigar factory where Luis works. Luis is arrested but freed on bond. When he comes back home, he finds Emelia gone. Subsequently, Luis receives a phone call from a bartender informing him that Emelia has been drinking and to come to pick her up. Emelia reveals to her brother that she had gone to see Silvera's wife to ask her to stop her husband from crucifying Luis. When Silvera returns home, his wife describes the encounter with Emelia. He tells her not to believe anything Emelia told her. Outside of the Silvera home, Luis again confronts the detective but then walks away upon seeing Mrs. Silvera staring out of a window.

Later that night, another detective comes to Luis' home and advises him that he has been cleared of the robbery charges. Mrs. Silvera had gone to police headquarters and informed them of her husband's actions. Detective Silvera is arrested after the drug addict he had blame Luis for the robbery recanted his story.

On February 10, 1960, Desi played a character named Chris Hunter operating a gambling casino in a North African town. "Thunder in the Night," by Sheldon Reynolds centers on a set of counterfeit passport printing plates and a group of underworld characters who are vying for them. A U.S. State Department agent attempting to locate the printing plates has already been murdered. A new agent, Bob Carter (Rod Taylor), has been sent to continue the investigation. Carter attempts to enlist Hunter in negotiating with Paul Reuter (George Macready) to obtain the plates. Reuter, a local underworld figure, is trying to purchase the plates from a Mr. Wilnow (Massimo Serato) who has been using them to print bogus American passports. Reuter is seeking to expand the counterfeit passport business. Initially, Hunter is not interested in assisting Carter. However, after Carter goes missing, Chris steps in to find his friend. Hunter is able to take the plates from one of Reuter's henchmen who was sent to steal them from Wilnow. Chris hopes to use the plates to obtain Carter's release. Carter turns up dead. While Reuter divulges that he had been holding Carter, he released him alive. Hunter then suspects that Wilnow had Carter murdered. In the end, Hunter shoots Wilnow.

Desilu filmed this episode entirely on location in Italy. *Variety* noted that "Arnaz looked in fine fettle, but could not give his peculiar role much substance..."[35]

Appearing as a character other than Lucy Ricardo on a November 17, 1958 stanza of the *Desilu Playhouse*, Lucille Ball starred as Kitty Winslow in "K. O. Kitty" written by Madelyn Martin and Bob Carroll, Jr. Her co-stars were William Lundigan as David Pierce, her boyfriend who is an attorney, and Aldo Ray as Harold Tibbets, a boxer. The episode's original title was "Pardon My Gloves."

Kitty is a dance teacher who learns that she has inherited a boxer bequeathed to her by her late Uncle Charlie. She thinks she is getting a dog and so is surprised when Harold Tibbets from Nebraska shows up at her door thinking that Kitty will be his new manager. David doesn't want Kitty to manage a boxer, but Tibbets has spent all his money traveling to Los Angeles to see Kitty.

While David is away on a business trip that, if successful, may make him a partner in his law firm and so will be able to marry Kitty, she decides to manage Harold. Kitty meets with a fight promoter to schedule Harold's first match and learns, at a gym, the different exercises boxers do to prepare for a fight, giving Lucille Ball an opportunity to display her physical comedy prowess. When Harold has problems performing the exercises, she decides to give him dance lessons to improve his foot work while

William Lundigan, Aldo Ray, and Lucille Ball in "K. O. Kitty."

singing "I Can't Give You Anything but Love, Baby." David arrives back from his trip unexpectedly and is jealous when he sees Harold and Kitty together. They argue with David leaving Kitty.

Come the night of the fight, Harold is knocked about the ring initially until Kitty begins singing "I Can't Give You Anything but Love, Baby" to remind him of his dance steps. Harold wins the match and goes on to knockout several subsequent opponents.

David tries one last time to get Kitty to give up the fight game by hiring two men from the gym to pose as mobsters to keep her away from Harold's next fight so she can't sing to the boxer. However, David learns that Harold plans to stop fighting after this match because he will have enough money to buy a farm in Nebraska. After Kitty informs her captors that this will be Harold's last fight, they take her to the arena for her to sing to Harold. Naturally, he wins the match, and presumably Harold returns to Nebraska to buy his farm and Kitty and David get married.

While Vivian Vance never appeared on an episode of *Desilu Playhouse* in a role other than herself, her co-star, William Frawley did. He played a Little League baseball coach named Joe Grady on a March 9, 1959 installment, "The Comeback," about his character's efforts to resurrect the career of a former big league baseball player.

In addition to the episodes starring Desi and Lucy, *The Desilu Playhouse* was the launching pad for two iconic series – *The Twilight Zone* and *The Untouchables*.

Airing in October 1958, "The Time Element," written by Rod Serling, was a pre-pilot for *The Twilight Zone*. That episode of the *Desilu Playhouse* starred William Bendix as Peter Jenson, a former bartender with a recurring dream. Jenson goes to a psychiatrist, Dr. Gillespie (Martin Balsam) to relate his troubling dream. Jenson's dream has him waking up in a hotel room from a hangover. Even though he fell asleep in a hotel in New York City in October 1958, he awakens in a room at the Imperial Hawaiian Hotel on December 6, 1941, the day before the Japanese attack on Pearl Harbor. At the hotel's bar, he meets a newlywed couple, the Jankowski's, where the husband (Darryl Hickman), an Ensign, is assigned to the USS Arizona. Believing that he really has traveled back in time, Jenson begins betting on sporting events that will take place in 1942 with knowledge of the winners.

After Ensign Jankowski visits his hotel room to see how he is doing with Jenson knowing that the sailor will be abroad the ship that will be sunk by the Japanese, Jenson contacts the local newspaper trying to explain to them about the impending bombing of Pearl Harbor. But the newspaper editor doesn't believe his story. Back at the hotel, he has another drink with the newlyweds and informs the Ensign about the pending attack. Not believing this, Jankowski punches him. Jenson regains consciousness in his hotel room the next morning as Japanese planes descend on the island. Jenson then wakes up from his dream, and it is 1958.

The psychiatrist attempts to come up with an explanation for Jenson's dream but doesn't convince him that it was only a fantasy. Jenson falls asleep on the psychiatrist's couch and again dreams he is in Hawaii in 1941. However, this time when he wakes up in his hotel room on the morning of December 7, he is killed by fire from the Japanese planes and his body disappears from Gillespie's couch. Gillespie doesn't know if he dreamed the encounter with Jenson or not. The doctor goes to a local bar and sees Jenson's picture on the wall. He is told that Jenson formerly tended bar at the establishment but was killed at Pearl Harbor.

Westinghouse through their ad agency, McCann-Erickson, had concerns about some scenes in the Rod Serling script. For example, the scene where the Jenson character goes to a newspaper to warn them of the impending attack on Pearl Harbor originally was to have the character trying to warn the Army about the bombing, but that branch of the service brushes him off as a crackpot. Since Westinghouse had several contracts with the Defense Department, they didn't want to show the Army in a bad light. Serling was asked to rewrite that scene.

At the end of the episode, Lucille Ball appears with her husband saying that she wanted to phone him during the show to tell him how good the episode was but that Betty Ramsey (the Ricardo's neighbor in Connecticut) was on the party line and Lucy couldn't get through. Lucy then plugs the upcoming *Lucille Ball-Desi Arnaz Show* starring Danny Thomas and his TV family from *The Danny Thomas Show*.

The pilot for *The Untouchables* aired in two parts on the *Desilu Playhouse*. Set in 1929 Chicago, the first episode began with the U.S. Justice Department wanting to stop Al Capone's criminal enterprises by either proving him guilty of income tax evasion or by shutting down his illegal breweries and distilleries. The Department contacts Eliot Ness to establish a special squad made up of seven honest Treasury agents – the "Untouchables" to target Capone's businesses. Since Capone is in prison in Philadelphia on firearm violations, Frank Nitti is running his empire. Ness' squad begins wrecking Capone's distilleries and then starts shutting down his breweries.

After serving ten months in prison, Al Capone is released and returns to Chicago. He vows to take care of Ness. Ness speaks to the newspapers about Capone's attempts to bribe him and his men and requests the public's help in destroying Capone's remaining business. Ness wants to knock off Capone's largest brewery near the Chicago stockyards but needs to find its exact location. Meanwhile, the mob attempts to murder Ness and succeeds in killing one of his agents. Capone turns himself in to authorities preempting his arrest for ordering the murder of the Treasury agent, but he has an airtight alibi. The hit man whom Capone hired to kill Ness and who murdered one of Ness' agents is murdered himself. Ness then goes after Capone's biggest brewery and phones the mob boss informing him that the establishment has been destroyed. The next day in front of the hotel where Capone is staying, Ness parades all the beer trucks his men have captured in their raids. The Feds charge Capone with income tax evasion. He is sentenced to a term of eleven years in prison.

So began the saga of *The Untouchables*, which aired on ABC for four seasons and was Desilu's biggest hit drama while Desi Arnaz was in charge of the company.

Other episodes of *Desilu Playhouse* served as pilots for proposed series that were never picked up by a network.

U.S. Air Force

Beginning in 1957, Mort Briskin sought to develop an adventure series about the Air Force. Beirne Lay Jr., who had co-authored *Twelve O'Clock High*, initially wrote two scripts for the project but was then replaced by Frank Moss. In early 1958, Desi Arnaz decided to discontinue production of a pilot and instead do one or two sixty-minute shows as part of *Desilu Playhouse*.

One episode of that anthology series did focus on a major in the Air Force, but the episode was written by Joseph Landon – not Frank Moss. Originally titled "Galaxy" and then "Man in Orbit," and based on a story, "The Cave of Night" by James Gunn, the installment dealt with a scientific team attempting to launch the first astronaut into orbit around Earth. The team, headed by Dr. Eric Carson (E.G. Marshall), an astrophysicist who dreams in exact mathematical formulas, consisted of Dr. Anthony Gambetta (Martin Balsam), another astrophysicist, and General Finch (Robert F. Simon), Chief of Public Relations for the Man in Space Project, as well as an aeronautical expert, an electronics engineer, and a medical doctor.

Dr. Carson has his doubts about Major David Roberts (Lee Marvin), the man selected to go into space since he is not a scientist. But Carson ultimately accepts Roberts for the assignment. First, the team launches a prototype rocket with a monkey on board, but the launch is not successful because of a malfunction with the navigation system. Dr. Carson believes that the launch schedule can be maintained, however, for the next launch with a man on board, by installing new gyros. The team plans to go with a fully simulated dry run as the next step.

During the dry run, Roberts convinces Carson and his team to really launch the rocket since everything is going well. The launch is a success, and the capsule goes into orbit. However, Roberts notifies mission control that the manual recovery control is not working meaning that he can't slow the craft for re-entry.

As the entire world listens to Roberts reporting on what Earth looks like from outer space, everyone comes together to try to get the astronaut back to the planet. Roberts' oxygen supply will run out in seven days. A decision is made to launch a second astronaut into space whose capsule will fly in front of Roberts' craft to slow it down and permit re-entry of both space vehicles. With less than seventy-two hours to go before Roberts' oxygen is depleted, the second rocket is launched with the hope that Air Force Major Roberts can be saved.

The organization, "Little People of America," evidently protested the casting of Lee Marvin in the role of the astronaut in this episode. Nela Nelson, vice president of the group, claimed that its members "beat their little knuckles raw on the 'Desilu Playhouse' casting office trying to get work in the studio's telepic..." Nelson went on to comment that, "Instead, they hired Lee Marvin, a huge, big giant who must weigh 200 pounds. He can't go far in any orbit."[36]

About "Man in Orbit," *Variety* wrote:

> Flushed by one success (sale of "The Untouchables" to ABC-TV), Desilu appears to be making a regular practice of using its Monday CBS-TV slot to audition hour-long telefilm prints for all three TV networks. In the Monday (11) morning N.Y. Times, the production house carried an ad alerting NBC, ABC and CBS to watch that night's "Westinghouse Desilu" show ... Particular stanza, luckily for the producer, was pretty good but whether it would make a running 60-minute series for next season or the season after may be still another story.[37]

The show business paper was correct in pointing out that Desilu couldn't launch Lee Marvin into space for the first time in every episode of a possible series. Nevertheless, the company could have been planning to make this series about the Air Force an anthology and not a continuing character drama.

Bandwagon

On January 26, 1959, Jane Russell starred in "Ballad for a Bad Man" (originally titled "Guns and Guitar"). Written by Bob Barbash from a story suggested by Desi Arnaz and directed by Jerry Hopper, the show also featured Steve Forrest as Chris Hody, a bounty hunter. Russell played Lilli Travers, a singer with the traveling entertainment troupe known as the "Barnaby Tibbs Bandwagon."

This project appears to have been an outgrowth from a 1958 proposal titled *Bandwagon*. *Bandwagon* was to be a period Western musical featuring six girls and a musical medicine man-type character. Arnaz had discussed with bandleader Harry James the possibility of him starring in this pilot.

In "Ballad for a Bad Man," the character of Lilli Travers is described as an attractive woman of about thirty who has a tough exterior but a sincere desire to help others. Lilli knows men but blames herself for the kind of life she led before becoming a singer with the Bandwagon. Her sister Amy (Karen Sharpe) is also a member of the troupe and is in love with Danny Cash (Roger Perry), who is wanted for bank robbery and the murder of a bank teller. Chris Hody (Steve Forrest) has been shadowing the troupe hoping to capture Cash who at one time was the Bandwagon's guide.

One night, Danny comes to the troupe's wagons to see Amy. He proclaims his innocence to Lilli of the crimes for which he is wanted. Members of the troupe create a diversion so Cash can escape capture by Hody and the town's sheriff. Hody then volunteers to guide the troupe as they travel through Indian Territory to their next town. Chris becomes infatuated with Lilli who discovers a wanted poster for Cash in his shirt and realizes why he wants to be with the troupe. Both Lilli and Barnaby Tibbs (Jack Haley) confront Hody about his plans to capture Danny Cash. Although they say that Danny never robbed the bank, Hody is not convinced. One night, when Hody sees Danny return to the wagons to meet

Amy, he realizes that he no longer has the heart to capture him. After Amy and Danny go off together, Lilli thanks Hody for letting them go.

Danny again returns to the troupe late at night to remove sideboards from a wagon to retrieve a canvas money bag. When he is discovered by one of the members of the troupe, Danny shoots him and flees with the bag. Chris tracks him down. Danny admits to the robbery and the murder as well as the shooting of a member of the Bandwagon. Chris and Danny have a shoot-out with Chris killing him. Chris decides to join the Bandwagon as its permanent guide.

After "Ballad for a Bad Man" was filmed, Desi Arnaz asked Russell to make another pilot playing the same character. Ms. Russell wasn't thrilled with the idea, saying ". . . I don't know if I want to or not. It's another western."[38] At the time, Jane Russell didn't really care if she had her own series. She was still under contract with Howard Hughes who was paying her $1000 a week for the next twenty years. And so, a Western series starring Jane Russell as a voluptuous singer never became a reality.

Nightclub

In 1959, Desi Arnaz attempted to finalize a deal with dancer/actress Cyd Charisse and her husband, singer/actor Tony Martin, for a thirty-minute drama titled *Nightclub* to be produced by Desilu for ABC. The series was to be based on a 1958 installment of *The Westinghouse-Desilu Playhouse* titled "Chez Rouge" written by Adrian Spies.

"Chez Rouge" was the name of a nightclub in Panama City co-owned by Mary (Janis Paige), nicknamed "The Redhead," who performed at the night spot. The club's motto was "The whole world comes to Chez Rouge." Her love interest, Paul, a pilot boat captain, had saved Mary from a gang rape in Mexico. In the episode, the police want to speak with Mary about her former husband, Robert Mason, who is involved with a revolution in San Marino. Mason wants to obtain money to buy serum to stop a typhoid epidemic among the insurgents. The police think that Mason will visit Chez Rouge to ask his ex-wife for the money. Mason does indeed come to the club, and Paul eventually talks Mary into giving her ex the money he needs.

The Cyd Charisse/Tony Martin series, *Nightclub*, never materialized.

Donegan's Six Guns

Another installment of *The Westinghouse/Desilu Playhouse* served as the basis for a potential family Western series. "Six Guns for Donegan," starring Lloyd Nolan as Sheriff Orville Darrow, aired October 16, 1959. The episode focused on a sheriff with arthritic hands dealing with the birth of a new daughter, a coward named Charlie (Harry Townes) that he is trying to protect, and his five sons who think of themselves as quick draw artists.

Charlie, a good-for-nothing townsman, has just been acquitted in the killing of one of the Clinton brothers. The sheriff promises his wife, Hilda (Jean Hagen), that he will get Charlie out of town so he won't have to protect him from the remaining four Clinton brothers. But Charlie keeps coming back to town. As a consequence, Darrow must face the brothers alone with everyone unaware that arthritis has crippled his gun hand. Darrow has to keep ordering his oldest son, Clay (James Franciscus), back home since he is eager to help his father. When the showdown with the Clinton's comes, Darrow's gun slips out of his hand when he draws, but Clay returns to face the Clinton's. When they are about to take him, up on nearby roofs are three of his siblings. In a store window with a shotgun is the fifth brother and inside the store is Mrs. Darrow. The Clinton's are convinced by an exhibition of sharpshooting by the Darrow family to ride out of town.

The idea of turning this *Desilu Playhouse* episode into a series was rejected in February 1960 but was resurrected again in 1963 by Jerry Thorpe. The second time around was not the charm, and the project was abandoned in September 1963.

Johnny Cinderella

Based on an installment from the *Westinghouse-Desilu Playhouse* titled "Murder Is a Private Affair," Desilu sought to make this episode a series for CBS about an adventurer in his thirties who, as a child, had been adopted by an older man. His adoptive father assigns him various investigations. The 1960 proposal was created by Frank Fenton and would have been a half-hour program.

The pilot starred David Brian as Mr. Bleeck, a man suffering from gout who had made millions as a professional gambler. He lives in a mansion with his staff, most notably Ingrid (Myrna Hansen), his secretary. Bleeck had adopted Johnny Cinderella (Adam West) after the boy's father, a cop, had been killed.

Bleeck is contacted about the whereabouts of a wealthy heiress who has checked herself into a seedy boarding house because of fear that her current husband, Hal Bannister (Peter Adams), is going to kill her since he needs money. Bleeck went to school with the woman's father. He has Ingrid contact Cinderella to help the woman – Aline Lincoln (Dina Merrill). Cinderella finds that Bannister lost $60,000 in a Las Vegas scam and needs funds to pay off his debt. Bannister is being followed by two henchmen from out of town – Hein and Cassady.

Johnny goes to Bannister's apartment and discovers him dead. Bleeck believes that Hein and Cassady murdered Bannister, but they claim innocence. Next, Bleeck thinks that Jan Revere (Barbara Hines), the cigarette girl from the Crown Room, a bar that Bannister frequented, might know something about his murder since he had been married to her. She confesses that she murdered Bannister. Apparently, he had never divorced her before marrying Aline Lincoln. She had wanted him to leave Aline and go away with her. When he refused, she killed him. Bleeck asks Cinderella to contact a lawyer to defend Revere saying that anyone who was connected with Bannister needs a break.

There were no further adventures of Johnny Cinderella, but Adam West did go on to star in a project that became a hit series – ABC's *Batman*.

Some websites, such as Internet Movie Database and the Classic TV Archive, list a show named *Dr. Kate* starring Jane Wyman as an episode of *Desilu Playhouse* that was an unsold pilot for a series. However, this author could find no confirmation that such a show ever aired on that series. *Dr. Kate*, based on the life of physician Kate Newcomb, focused on a general practitioner treating patients in the small town of Boulder Junction, Colorado. In the 1960 pilot script, written by Harry Essex, Kate and her husband Bill attempt to befriend a young girl named Lucy whose pregnant mother was wounded when police arrested Lucy's father. Lucy has a younger brother who is deaf. Kate tries to help both the out-of-control Lucy and her brother while their mother is in the hospital.

While evidently *Dr. Kate* did not air on *Desilu Playhouse*, there is a small article in the July 19, 1961 edition of *Variety* that ABC planned to broadcast the pilot as a special in October 1961.

Chapter 9: Unsold Kraft Mystery Theatre Spin-offs

When, after its second season, *Desilu Playhouse* was not renewed by CBS, Desilu aired repeats of eight episodes of that anthology under the title of *Kraft Mystery Theatre*, a summer replacement series for NBC's *The Perry Como Show* in 1962. In addition to the repeats, Desilu produced eight new mystery episodes representing the first time the production company sold a series to NBC.

Two of the new episodes represented pilots for potential series.

Dr. Augustus Van Dusen Mysteries

Based on a story by Jacques Futrelle called "The Problem in Cell No. 13," this unsold pilot for a planned mystery series aired as an August 29, 1962 episode of *Kraft Mystery Theatre*. Claude Dauphin appeared as professor Dr. Augustus Van Dusen, a criminologist nicknamed "The Thinking Machine," who bets Warden Harry Gough (Everett Sloane) that he can escape from a maximum security prison cell in seven days. The challenge is placed after the two argue over how best to spend state budget money either on criminal reform or more maximum security facilities. Dr. Van Dusen contends that a prison hasn't been built that is escape proof.

Augustus enters the cell in Gough's prison with newly polished shoes, two $10 bills, a $5 bill, and a can of toothpowder. Soon he is sending out notes written in ink, his money has changed from large denominations to small denominations, and a man in a nearby cell is taken out screaming because he hears voices in the night. A few days after his incarceration, a guard sees Augustus sawing at the bars on his cell window. The warden has cell 13 searched and finds the file Augustus was using. At night, a prisoner named Joseph Ballard is screaming that he is hearing voices mentioning "acid." Despite entering the prison with only one $5 bill and

Stafford Repp as a prison guard and Everett Sloane as Warden Harry Gough in "The Problem in Cell No. 13."

two $10 bills, the professor tosses fifty-cent pieces from his window to the guards and is found with five $1 bills in his cell.

On the seventh day of his imprisonment, Dr. Van Dusen informs the guard to expect a message from him every two hours until he escapes his cell. A colleague of Van Dusen's, a Dr. Slater, comes by to pick him up. When the power to one area of the prison goes out, an emergency crew from the electric company arrives to restore the power. After the electricity is back on, the guard finds Augustus missing from his cell. Van Dusen enters the warden's office posing as a photographer with his friend Hutchinson Hatch, a newspaper reporter, whom the warden had called to witness that the professor was unable to escape his cell.

Later, at his home, Van Dusen explains how he was able to escape. Through a drain hole in his cell where rats from a nearby recreation field outside the prison were hiding, the professor captured a rat and unraveled a string from his socks tying one end of the string to the leg of the rat. He pushed the rodent into the drain with a note and a $10 bill tied to the string about twelve inches from the animal's leg. Van Dusen used the end of his shoe laces and polish from his shoes to pen the note. The animal ran to the nearest outlet gnawing off the string. Luckily a child near the outlet playing in the field outside the prison found the money and the note which read: "This ten dollars belongs to the finder. If he takes this note to Hutchinson Hatch, he will receive another ten dollars."

To the rest of the string left in the drainpipe by the rat, Hatch tied a stronger cord that Van Dusen would pull into his cell through the drain opening with materials like acid and small denominations of money that he could use. The professor used the acid to cut through the steel bars on his window with the tooth powder acting to buffer the acid. He used a long electric cord tipped with nitric acid to cut the wires providing electricity to one area of the facility in which his cell was located. Hatch masqueraded as one member of the crew that came to the prison to restore the power. While the electricity was out, Van Dusen removed the bars from his window and crawled out of the window to the power company's vehicle to hide until electricity was restored. Hatch then took him to the warden's office.

If the pilot had been picked up as a series, more mysteries written by Jacques Futrelle featuring Professor Van Dusen would have served as the basis for the episodes. In the 1900s, Futrelle wrote several stories highlighting the exploits of the professor including *The Problem of the Auto Cab*, *The Problem of Dressing Room A*, and *The Problem of the Vanishing Man*.

Duncan Maclain Mysteries

Initially titled "Blind Detective" and then "Man from Blue Fox," this episode, "Change of Heart," based on the novels by Baynard Kendrick, concerned a blind private eye and his seeing-eye dog. Desilu initially discussed doing the pilot either as a thirty-minute or a one-hour show but settled on the latter. The pilot episode aired September 12, 1962 on *Kraft Mystery Theatre*.

Robert Middleton starred as blind detective Duncan Maclain. Donald May was featured as Maclain's assistant, and Russ Conway played the police inspector.

The pilot had Maclain investigating a series of fatal falls from high places in seemingly deserted buildings which the detective concludes are really murders. He solves the case by offering himself as bait for the murderer.

Kendrick wrote several mystery novels about the exploits of Duncan Maclain, which served as the basis for two 1940s motion pictures – *Eyes in the Night* and *The Hidden Eye*, starring actor Edward Arnold.

Chapter 10: The Untouchables Inspired Unsold Pilots

Starring Robert Stack as Prohibition agent Eliot Ness, *The Untouchables*, ran for four seasons on ABC from October 1959 to September 1963. The series was based on a book co-authored by Ness about how he formed a team of federal agents to take down infamous mobster Al Capone in Chicago in the 1930s. Known for its depictions of mob violence, the series' ratings diminished when NBC counter-programmed *The Untouchables* with *Sing Along with Mitch* starring Mitch Miller.

Desilu attempted to use *The Untouchables* as a launch pad for other dramas as delineated below.

C.I.C. (Counter-Intelligence Corps)

In October 1960, producer Josef Shaftel received permission to develop this series about the Counter-Intelligence Corps spanning from World War II to the 1960s. The project was envisaged as *The Untouchables* for that era. Desi made a deal with NBC for two one-hour specials to launch the series for the 1961-62 season. When the deal with that network didn't work out, ABC aired the two specials on September 23 and 30, 1961.

The pilot, titled "The Assassination Plot at Teheran," starred John Larch as the C.I.C. agent, Dan York. Based on a rumor which had some currency at the 1943 Teheran Conference, the pilot dealt with a plan by Adolf Hitler, in partnership with his Axis followers, to assassinate Roosevelt, Churchill, and Stalin during the conference.

William Spier developed three treatments for episodes of the series. One, "Operation Waterfront" concerned the sabotage of a luxury liner being converted to a Naval vessel for the war effort. Dan York and his C.I.C. agents are called to New York City to investigate the sabotage. They determine that the saboteurs escaped from the burning vessel by

The real Eliot Ness who died on May 16, 1957 before the pilot for The Untouchables *premiered.*

submarine and that some Americans on the waterfront not only assisted them but were also providing supplies to German subs attacking the Allied convoys in the Atlantic.

One of York's men named Mancini is kidnapped by the saboteurs when he is seen with the girlfriend of the main suspect, Larry Apollo. York and another agent find Mancini and free him, but Apollo escapes. Mancini identifies Apollo as a boy whom he knew when growing up in Hell's Kitchen. Apollo is killed by Nazis before the C.I.C. can arrest him. When Apollo's brother grants the C.I.C. all the necessary credentials to gain entrance to waterfront operations, the fishing fleet providing assistance to the Nazis is exposed.

With Robert Tallman, Spier developed another treatment for the planned series called "Operation Greif: The Eisenhower Abduction Plot." After the D-Day invasion, Hitler plotted to kidnap General Dwight Eisenhower, the head of Allied forces, and fly him to Berlin. In German, "greif" means to grasp or to hold. Hitler designated Otto Skorzeny, whom the C.I.C. dubbed the most dangerous man in Europe, and Hans Von Frischen, Chief of Espionage, to carry out the plan. Von Frischen was to gain information about Eisenhower's daily schedule, while Skorzeny would train German soldiers to impersonate GI's.

Dan York suspects that the new laundress at Eisenhower's headquarters may be a Nazi spy. When the C.I.C. finds her passing notes to Von Frischen, York and his men capture her and the Chief of Espionage. Agents also discover that Von Frischen was seen with Skorzeny. Skorzeny goes ahead with his plan despite knowing that Von Frischen has been arrested. He plots to kidnap Eisenhower when the general enters Paris to celebrate its liberation. Skorzeny and his men place time bombs on the route Eisenhower will take into the city. Posing as a U.S. Security Officer, he informs officials at the French War Office that he caught men placing the bombs and suggests that the general's route into Paris be switched. York learns of this and understands that the hotel in which the general will be staying is being changed. When Skorzeny nears Eisenhower's hotel suite after the general arrives in Paris, York and his men attempt to grab Skorzeny interrupting his kidnapping plans, but Skorzeny escapes. Presumably if *C.I.C.* had been picked up as a series, more episodes would have dealt with Otto Skorzeny.

The third treatment, "Operation: Bernhard," was developed as a possible two-part story. A German agent, Dr. Ernst Grobl, hires a burglar to steal a special linen paper from the Porter Paper Mill in Whitchurch, England. At British Intelligence, Dan York learns the story of the Whitchurch burglary. The paper that was stolen is the type the Bank of England uses to print money. British authorities conclude that Ernst Grobl, who hired the second-story man, is a Nazi agent.

In Berlin, the paper is given to Captain Bernhard Kruger, a specialist in the hoaxing and defrauding arts. To obtain maximum secrecy for the project, Kruger wants to set up a counterfeiting operation in a concentration camp. The Nazis first need to duplicate the quality of the paper before printing the bogus money – both American dollars and British pounds.

York and his agents travel to Ireland - the place where they believe Dr. Grobl has gone. Posing as Nazi agents, they visit a German agent who informs them about Captain Kruger.

Meanwhile, in Germany, Grobl locates an expert artist in an Austrian concentration camp who can assist with the counterfeiting. The plan goes forward with the plates being engraved by Solomon Smolianoff, the concentration camp victim that Grobl had found.

York deduces that the counterfeiting operation is taking place at Sachaenhausen Concentration Camp. Under cover of night, C.I.C. agents parachute into a forest clearing a few kilometers from the concentration camp. Heinrich Himmler, the Nazi Chief of the German Police and Minister of the Interior, visits the camp to monitor the progress on the plan. York and his men see a truck delivering a shipment of paper to one of the buildings in the camp and so determine where the counterfeiting operation is taking place.

A few days later, Grobl visits the camp to inform Kruger that Hitler has given the go ahead to print $300 million in dollars and a like amount in pounds. When he departs the camp, Grobl is captured by the C.I.C. York and his men mention their plans to destroy the camp in front of Grobl and then allow him to escape so he can inform Himmler of the plans. Himmler issues orders for the entire counterfeiting operation to be moved. After contacting London for reinforcements, York and Allied forces destroy the trucks carrying the plates, printers, and paper, free the concentration camp victims working on the project, and capture Bernhard Kruger.

The White Knights

In 1960, Mort Briskin came up with the concept of a series about a team of doctors, affiliated with the public health service, who operate internationally. His idea was to play up suspense and action and play down clinical aspects. Briskin hoped to get four top names to star. Among those under consideration for the roles were Walter Pidgeon, Farley Granger, and Thomas Mitchell.

By 1961, after CBS had passed on the series, Desilu shopped it to ABC. In 1962, Briskin sold his interest in the project to Desilu. The planned series was envisioned as a spin-off from *The Untouchables*. Set in the 1930s, two pilots were made, both with Dane Clark and John Gabriel as the leads. The first pilot, "Bird in the Hand," aired October 30, 1962 on *The Untouchables*; the second, "Jake Dance," was broadcast on January 22, 1963.

"Bird in the Hand" was set in 1929 Chicago where mobster Arnie Kurtz (Carroll O'Connor) is being surveilled by Ness and his men. Kurtz has his wife Stella instruct her brother Benno Fisk, a pawn shop owner and bird fancier, to deliver $100,000 in cash to Kurtz's partner in Washington D.C. Unbeknownst to him, Fisk has contracted parrot fever from his birds. While Fisk is traveling to Washington, his sister takes care of the birds. Upon arriving in D.C., Fisk passes out but not before hiding the satchel with the money. He is taken to the hospital near death. Dr. Victor Garr (Clark) and his assistant Dan Gifford (Gabriel), both of the U.S. Public Health Service, are contacted. Dr. Garr interviews Fisk who tells him that his sister has the birds in Chicago. Dr. Gifford flies to Chicago where he locates the hotel in which the Kurtz's are staying. But, after a fight with her husband, Stella has left the hotel, and her husband flees when Gifford informs him about the birds.

Gifford finds a patient suffering from the fever in Cook County Hospital. Other patients with the disease are admitted to the facility as the doctor attempts to find a common thread among them. He deduces that they all visited Fisk's pawn shop in Chicago. Gifford goes to the shop and finds Stella dead. Meanwhile, Kurtz travels to Washington to deliver another $100,000 to his partner since the money bag Fisk was to deliver ends up in the hands of the police. The Public Health Service spreads word about parrot fever in the Washington area. After seeing the news, Kurtz contacts a doctor at the hotel where he is staying under an assumed name. The doctor phones Dr. Garr. Kurtz goes to the Lincoln Memorial to drop off the money to his partner. The partner provides Kurtz with a list of all the distilleries and contacts in Chicago in exchange for the money. They are both arrested by Ness.

The second pilot, the "Jake Dance," dealt with a medication called "ginger jake" that contains alcohol but causes tremors and paralysis in people who drink it. Dane Clark and John Gabriel reprise their roles on this episode, in addition to Joseph Schildkraut appearing as Hans Frolick. They investigate cases of the jake dance in Wichita, Kansas. Meanwhile, in Chicago, Eliot Ness is called in when twenty-one barrels of hair tonic are stolen. Ness is concerned that the hair tonic will be mixed with ginger jake to make it taste better for public consumption as an alcoholic beverage. Ness contacts the U.S. Public Health Service about his concerns.

A young woman is admitted to a Cook County hospital with signs of ingesting ginger jake. After Dr. Gifford informs her that 1200 people have been paralyzed from the medication and that she will probably never recover from its effects, she divulges that she purchased ginger jake from her uncle, a local pharmacist. The pharmacist is arrested along with one of the mobsters behind the theft of the hair tonic. Ness allows the mobster to escape custody so that he will lead them to his boss who turns out to be the owner of the hair tonic factory.

Dr. Gifford apologizes to the young woman for upsetting her about the effects of the medication, and the Public Health Service closes down the lab making the poison.

Commenting on this back-door pilot and the one profiled next, Arnaz remarked, "I don't like spinoffs unless the show involved fits into the series on which it's seen. We don't want to weaken 'The Untouchables,' but these two properties did integrate into the series."[39]

The Seekers

In *The Seekers*, Barbara Stanwyck played Lt. Agatha Stewart of the Chicago Police Department's Missing Person's Bureau in the 1930's. Two episodes of *The Untouchables* served as pilots for the drama. The first airing November 20, 1962 titled "Elegy" concerned a racketeer, Charley Radick (John Larch), dying of cancer, who wants to see his long-lost daughter. Ness is afraid that Radick's death will prompt a gang war over control of the gangster's rackets and so makes a deal with Radick that he will find his daughter if the racketeer turns over his books to him. Ness contacts Aggie to locate the daughter. Aggie is assisted by Det. Frank Benson (Ed Asner). Her secretary is June played by African-American actress Virginia Capers.

Tough, no nonsense Stewart eventually finds Margaret Radick (Peggy Ann Garner) and has her reunite with her father who by now is in a hospital. Radick turns over his records to Ness.

The second episode featuring the Aggie Stewart character aired on January 1, 1963 and was titled "Search for a Bad Man." In the episode, Stewart attempts to find the identity of a dead man found floating in Lake Michigan. Meanwhile, Eliot Ness investigates a $1 million shipment of illegal liquor from Canada to Chicago. Stewart discovers that the body found in the lake was that of gangster Jake Portuguese, who was behind the illegal liquor smuggling. His brother Rudy dumped the body in the lake after Jake had a heart attack. He wanted to keep his brother's death a secret until he got the liquor and sold it for $1 million. In the end, Rudy is killed in a shoot-out with Ness and his men.

This was one of the last projects Desi Arnaz approved before he retired from the presidency of Desilu. Production was completed in mid-September 1962. Although the pilots were set in the 1930s, if ABC had picked up its option on the show it would have been a contemporary series.

Floyd Gibbons: Reporter

Scott Brady starred as newspaper reporter Floyd Gibbons in this unsold spin-off from *The Untouchables* airing December 11, 1962. The real Floyd Gibbons was an active, colorful reporter covering stories all over the world. Leonard Freeman and Alvin Cooperman developed the project.

In the "Floyd Gibbons Story," Gibbons, wearing a white eyepatch since he had lost an eye during World War I, comes to Chicago and sees a newspaper headline that a journalist acquaintance of his, Carl Edmunds, has been murdered. Edmunds had been working on a story about the syndicate infiltrating the scrap metal business and shipping the metal overseas. The syndicate is seeking to diversify its business since the mob believes that Prohibition will soon be repealed.

A member of the syndicate, Vince Dastille (Joseph Campanella), had Edmunds killed before the reporter could publish his story. The head of the syndicate, John Brecker (Alan Baxter) considers Dastille a loose cannon. Gibbons volunteers to help Ness in his investigation of Edmunds murder, but Ness refuses his assistance. Gibbons starts his own inquiry. He surmises that Edmunds' widow, Kitty (Dorothy Malone), who wanted to divorce her husband, was having an affair with Dastille since she previously worked at his nightclub. After Gibbons begins his own inquiry into the mob's involvement in the scrap metal business, Dastille orders a hit on the journalist which is vetoed by Brecker. Dastille is shot by Brecker's men after disagreeing about how the mob now wants to do business. Gibbons visits Brecker to inform him that he will publish the story Edmunds was writing revealing that the mob is selling scrap metal to the Nazis. Brecker attempts to bribe Gibbons into not publishing the article by giving him $50,000 which Gibbons takes as Ness' men arrive at Brecker's office. Ness' agents take care of Brecker's henchmen, while Ness shoots Brecker. Gibbons gives the $50,000 to Ness for the police charity.

The real Floyd Gibbons, who died at the age of fifty-two in 1939, had a career with the *Chicago Tribune* as well as with NBC radio.

The Con Man

Also titled *The Big Con*, this 1962 Desilu project for ABC dealt with classic con games – a different confidence scheme would be profiled each week. The series would be an anthology with no continuing characters.

The pilot for *The Con Man* appears to have been a January 8, 1963 episode of *The Untouchables* titled "The Speculator," guest starring Telly Savalas as Leo Stazak, the new bookkeeper for Frank Nitti. Leo gets in Nitti's good graces by defending him in front of Eliot Ness.

Nitti holds a meeting with all the mob bosses from the different territories and recommends that they agree to a massive smuggling operation bringing in booze from Canada. To execute the plan, $1.25 million is needed. Not all of the bosses agree to go forward, but Nitti decides to proceed anyway. To raise the needed cash, Stazak advises Nitti that he can double the mobster's money by investing it in the stock market. Nitti gives Leo hundreds of thousands of dollars which Stazak has no intention of actually investing. Instead, he has a printer make up bogus stock certificates in case Nitti wants to see what Stazak has spent the money on.

Ness, having surveilled the print shop, executes a search warrant and finds "proofs" of the stock certificates. The following day, the newspapers report a stock market crash. Leo thinks he sees a way of keeping Nitti's money by telling him that it was all lost in the crash. To spare his life from Nitti's wrath, Stazak comes up with an alternative plan for smuggling the Canadian booze into the United States. In the meantime, Ness questions the printer who shows the T-man the bogus certificates. Ness then visits Nitti to show him the certificate proofs. When Leo later visits Nitti, the mobster demands his money be returned. Leo attempts to blame the entire scam on his cousin whom he has murdered. After Stazak leaves Nitti, Ness follows him, confiscates Nitti's money from Leo, and arrests him.

Chapter 11: Desilu's Unsold Kid and Game Show Pilots

The only Desilu comedy to be syndicated was also the company's only project aimed at juveniles to become a series. *This Is Alice*, produced by Desilu and Sidney Salkow, was syndicated by NTA beginning in 1958. Patty Ann Gerrity starred as Alice Holliday, a nine-year old who was always trying to help people. She lived in River Glen, Georgia with her father Chet (Tommy Farrell) and mother Clarissa Mae (Phyllis Coates).

Variety described the series thusly in a review of an early episode: "'This Is Alice' is so-so fare that will appeal mostly to less discriminating juveniles and parents who envision film careers for their moppets... the viewer is presented with what the producers apparently felt was a lovable little girl who goes lovably about fixing the lives of basically lovable older people, but who actually is a very dull little girl who ought to confine her energies to hopscotch and hide-and-seek with the neighborhood children."

The review went on to state: "... Patty Ann Gerrity who is a good-looking and probably charming little girl in everyday life, is directed poorly by Sidney Salkow ... Salkow has Miss Gerrity speak so jarringly loud that frequently her words become entirely inarticulate. In addition, the moppet over-emotes throughout, and since she is the key figure in this series, the whole thing collapses under the burden of her obvious dramatics."[40]

Desilu sought to launch other series aimed at juveniles but without success.

Jon Whiteley/Vincent Winter Project

The two young stars of the movie, *The Little Kidnappers*, were being considered by Desilu for their own situation comedy in 1955. They would play British orphans adopted by American foster-parents. Actor Eddie Albert was under consideration for the role of the father.

The motion picture, *The Little Kidnappers*, concerned Harry and Davey, grandsons of a Scotsman living in Nova Scotia, who are forbidden by their grandfather from having a dog. And so, they "kidnap" an unattended baby and take care of the infant.

Apparently, no pilot for this Desilu project was filmed. After their careers as child actors ended, both Whiteley and Winter pursued other endeavors. Whiteley became an art historian; Winter, an assistant director.

Rikki of the Islands (aka Jungle Boy)

This unsold 1957 pilot centered on the adventures of an eleven-year-old boy (Ricky Vera) in the jungle, sort of a tropical Tom Sawyer. The locale for the planned series was to be Borneo or Sumatra although the show would have been filmed in Hollywood.

Ricky Vera, who had been discovered by Hoagy Carmichael, appeared on several episodes of *Our Miss Brooks* as Benny Romero. *Our Miss Brooks* starring Eve Arden was filmed at Desilu but not produced by that company.

Rikki of the Islands was a possibility for syndication but never became a series.

The only other children's series in which Desilu was involved was one titled *Desilu's Little People*. The company had set up its own syndication branch – Desilu Sales, Inc. in 1962 to distribute series produced by other companies. One of these series, made in Europe, was advertised to TV stations in the States as *Desilu's Little People*. The series featured puppets dramatizing various classic children's tales with narration for each episode done by a guest star. The unsold pilot, done in color, relayed the story of "Ali Baba and the Forty Thieves."

Turning to Desilu's production of game shows, in 1962, the company entered the field of live- on-tape game shows in partnership with producers Ralph Andrews and Bill Yagermann. Their one big success was the series *You Don't Say* which ran on NBC and then ABC for a number of years beginning in 1963.

Andrews and Yagermann along with Desilu had a unique approach to presenting these shows. Instead of making a pilot and shopping it around to the networks, they premiered their game shows on Los Angeles TV station KTLA to iron out any kinks in the format and to gauge network interest in picking up the series.

You Don't Say began on KTLA on November 25, 1962 with Jack Barry as the host. Tom Kennedy became emcee when the series moved to NBC. The original format had two teams consisting of a celebrity and a studio contestant. Each team attempted to guess names of famous people and places using incomplete sentences as clues. The last word in the sentence was supposed to sound like part of the name to be guessed.

While not technically "unsold" pilots, the following two shows produced by Desilu and Andrews and Yagermann never aired on any network – only on KTLA:

By the Numbers

On this series, two teams each made up of a celebrity and a contestant competed to make words from a thirty-character game board consisting of each letter of the alphabet and four blanks. The letters and blanks on the board were revealed to the teams for fifteen seconds and then the board was covered by numbers. Teams then picked numbers to reveal the letters underneath until one team spelled out a more than two letter word scoring ten points for each letter.

After spelling out a word, the team would start over to spell out more words until it passed to the other team, failed to make a proper word, or uncovered one of the four blanks. The first team earning 150 points won the game.

The show started on KTLA in late July 1962 with Jay Stewart as the host. In late January 1963, Jack Barry became the emcee with Wink Martindale replacing him in July 1963.

Zoom

Wink Martindale also hosted this once-a-week nighttime game show on KTLA beginning in July 1963 that failed to be picked up by a network.

On the show, contestants were asked to identify an object that had been magnified 300 times by a zoom camera lens called a "micro-televiser."

Relatively Yours

A brief article appeared in the January 26, 1966 issue of *Variety* that read as follows: "An audience participation game show, a joint venture of

Desilu Productions and producer Monty Hall, will be auditioned at CBS-TV Thursday as a possible replacement for 'The Lucy Show,' which stars Desilu prexy Lucille Ball."[41] This project did not involve Andrews and Yagermann as did the ones described above.

The game show was tentatively titled *Relatively Yours*, presumably a show involving family relationships. The reference to it being a replacement for Lucille Ball's comedy probably meant as a summer series to preempt reruns of *The Lucy Show*. No further details could be found about this project.

Chapter 12: Desilu's Unproduced Lucy Movies and TV Specials

Desi and Lucy's Movie Plans

As noted in the Preface, one of Lucy and Desi's goals in creating Desilu was to make movies. In the early 1950s, several features described below were considered by the couple but only one – *The Star*, came to fruition and that one ultimately didn't feature Ms. Ball nor was it produced by Desilu.

Blazing Beulah from Butte

Shortly after forming the company, the Arnaz's announced that they would be making a comedy film titled *Blazing Beulah from Butte* to be written and directed by Edward Sedgwick. Sedgwick was credited with discovering Ms. Ball and had worked as a director starting from the silent era of movies to the advent of television, including directing *I Love Lucy*.

The feature to be made in Technicolor concerned a Mexican played by Desi who comes to the United States looking for a cultured woman to marry. Instead of a refined lady, his character is hooked by Beulah, a rambunctious redhead character to be portrayed by Lucy, from Butte, Montana. While a copy of the proposed screenplay could not be found, evidently plans were to film some portions of Lucy and Desi's vaudeville act at the Roxy Theater to insert into the movie showing Beulah watching the stage show.

The Butte Chamber of Commerce had been after the couple to film the entire picture in Montana. The Chamber didn't realize that the story was about a woman who hates Butte and spends her entire life trying to leave the place.

Venus Mahoney

An idea for a movie called *Venus Mahoney* starring Lucille Ball was proposed by director Lloyd Bacon and his wife in spring 1950. The planned film told the story of a woman with an inferiority complex who becomes a fight manager and gets involved with gangsters. The premise seems very similar to the "K. O. Kitty" episode of *Desilu Playhouse* described in Chapter 8. Unknown is what role Desi may have had in the film. The Bacon's also considered singer Dinah Shore for the lead role instead of Lucy.

Apparently, plans for the movie never materialized. But according to information found among the Lloyd Bacon papers at the Margaret Herrick Library, the Bacon's later thought of turning *Venus Mahoney* into a television series.

Instead of becoming a fight manager, the initial treatment for the TV show dealt with Maggy Mahoney and her on again, off again love affair with her beau David Barnes, a garage mechanic. Maggy, who worked in the Household Department at Macy's in New York, was the main financial support for her family – Hap, her father; Bertie, her aunt who loved to knit; Arnold, her unemployed brother and his family including Gertrude his wife and Peter, his son; and Dinah, Maggy's teenage sister.

Maggy keeps postponing her wedding to Dave due to various family emergencies. Dave becomes frustrated and breaks off his relationship with her for a brief time causing Maggy to begin dating other men, including a wealthy bachelor, Palmer Woodruff. When Dave learns of Maggy's relationship with Woodruff, he begins dating his boss's daughter, Georgia. Both Maggy and Georgia compete in a bathing beauty contest to choose the Venus of Brighton Beach with Maggy winning the contest. Maggy and Dave then reconcile and announce that finally they will marry.

The Star

This drama project, written by Dale and Katherine Eunson, dealt with the fading career of a Hollywood movie star. The main character, Margaret Elliot, is bankrupt and attempting a comeback in films. She refuses to face the fact that her days as a lead actress are over. She is offered a role in a new project about an actress who cannot accept her declining popularity and comes to realize that her movie career is finally at an end.

Reportedly, the Eunson's based the Margaret Elliot character on the career of Joan Crawford. When plans for Lucille Ball to star in the film did not come to fruition, Bette Davis took the role. *The Star* was released in late 1952.

That Townsend Girl

Elaine Townsend (born Margaret Helgeson in 1919) was a successful entrepreneur in the 1940s. Arriving in Cuba in 1947, she purchased the dice concession at the Grand Casino National in Havana. A year or so later, the government-owned casino was shut down, but not before Townsend had sold her interest in it. Townsend then partnered with Cuban Efron J. Pertierra and purchased two former casinos. The casinos dominated Havana's gaming industry.

In an interview with columnist Bob Thomas in late 1949, Townsend recalled, "I was born in the little town of Powell, Wyo. I went to the University of Denver and I taught at a commercial school in Denver. Finally, I got so cold I took a trip to Honolulu." She went on to remark, "When I went back home, I was colder than ever. So I took another trip -this time to Havana. I stayed at the National Hotel and out by the pool I would hear all the big-money talk. I happened to hear that the chemin de fer (a French card game also known as 'shimmy') and crap concession at the hotel was open, so I snapped it up."[42]

One of Townsend's clients was screenwriter Virginia Kellogg who wrote a screenplay about Elaine's life. The proposed movie, alternately titled *The Elaine Townsend Story*, *Hotbed in Cuba*, and *That Townsend Girl*, to be directed by Wolfgang Reinhardt, was to be a comedy about Townsend's life starring Rita Hayworth. When Hayworth became pregnant, Reinhardt sought out Lucille Ball to star as Townsend with Desi Arnaz co-starring. But the film was never made.

Lucy's Solo Possibilities

After ending *I Love Lucy* as a regular weekly half-hour series, Lucy and Desi continued to appear in one-hour *I Love Lucy* specials titled *The Lucille Ball-Desi Arnaz Show* and also starred on some special episodes of the *Desilu Playhouse* as previously described.

News outlets reported in late 1959 that Lucy and Desi were considering divorce. The couple filmed one last hour-length *Lucille Ball-Desi Arnaz*

Show in March 1960 – "Lucy Meets the Mustache" with Ernie Kovacs and his wife Edie Adams. Right after making that special, Lucille Ball announced divorce proceedings.

A January 18, 1960 Desilu Inter-Department Communication from Dorothy Hechtlinger to Bert Granet, subject: "Lucy Solo Possibilities," outlined several suggestions for Lucille Ball specials – none of which were ever made. Hechtlinger, at the time, was the story editor for *Desilu Playhouse*, and Bert Granet was a long-time producer for the company. The potential specials were evidently ideas for episodes of *Desilu Playhouse*, which was in its final season.

The suggestions ranged from a Madelyn Pugh Martin and Bob Carroll, Jr. script titled "Bride of the Month," information about which could not be found, to a topic labeled "Henry VIII idea," probably about a comic take-off on the English king with Lucy either playing each of his six wives or else appearing as the king. Other suggestions included "Lucy Boat Story" with an outline to be developed by writer Devery Freeman, which was rejected because the project was too similar to another one called "Landlubbers." Jerry Stagg, who helped produce *The Texan* and episodes of *Desilu Playhouse*, had an idea for Ms. Ball to star in a special called "Clown Story" or "Carnival," while Frank Gabrielson, who had written several episodes of the 1950s dramady *Mama*, had a script titled "Penny Candy," which Hechtlinger thought suitable for Lucy's talents.

Following is a description of the other proposals listed in the memorandum.

By the Beautiful Sea

In the TV adaptation of this 1954 Broadway musical written by Herbert and Dorothy Fields with music by Arthur Schwartz, Lucy would have appeared as Lottie Gibson, a vaudeville performer who, with her father, owns a theatrical boarding house by the sea on Coney Island. Lottie is in love with Shakespearian actor Dennis Emery. She persuades him to room in her boarding house where, just so happens, his divorced wife and daughter, known as "Baby Betsy" although she is seventeen, are residing. In order to win child parts on the stage, Betsy's mother instructs her daughter to dress as a thirteen-year-old.

Lottie wants to lend money to Dennis to help him out of his financial straits but finds that her father Carl has invested the money in a Coney

Island attraction. Lottie decides to win the prize for making a parachute jump from a balloon on the 4th of July. One can readily envisage Lucille Ball performing such a stunt. She did eventually do a skydiving scene on a September 21, 1971 episode of *Here's Lucy*.

In disguise, Lottie wins the prize, but the money is not enough. However, her father also wins money for being shot out of a cannon, and so she ends up with the funds she needs.

Baby Betsy, out of jealousy, tries to break up the romance between her father and Lottie. Intuitively, Lottie presents Betsy with one of her dresses. When Betsy puts it on, she looks seventeen and thanks Lottie. Lottie and Betsy go off to the midway together where Betsy is romanced by Mickey, a singing waiter, and Lottie by Dennis.

By Jupiter!

Set in the land of Amazon women, this musical by Rodgers and Hart involves an army of Greek soldiers arriving on the island of Pontus to acquire the sacred girdle of Diana from around the waist of Queen Hippolyta, the queen of the Amazon women. The Greek army's advance party is led by Theseus and war correspondent Homer. Theseus and Homer demand the girdle, but Hippolyta refuses to turn it over and throws them out of the palace. Theseus manages to sneak back to the palace to flirt with Antiope, Hippolyta's huntress sister.

When a messenger announces that the entire army of Greeks is coming to the island, Hippolyta marries Sapiens, the son of an arms dealer, in order to obtain the necessary equipment from his mother to fight the Greeks. A Greek delegation enters the palace bringing a personal challenge from Hercules, who is with the army, to Queen Hippolyta. Hippolyta trades girdles with her sister so that Hercules cannot steal the sacred one from her.

Hercules is terrified by Antiope and takes refuge in Sapiens' tent, while Antiope and Theseus fight. Antiope kisses Theseus thereby ending the conflict with Theseus carrying her off not realizing that she is wearing the sacred girdle. When Hippolyta realizes that the girdle is gone, Sapiens leads the fight to get it back. Sapiens goes to the Greek encampment where he is entranced by more feminine women at the camp. Sapiens retrieves the girdle and wears it in public. Now as King of the Amazons, he presents the girdle to Hercules.

Of all the specials described in this section, *By Jupiter!* was the closest to actually being produced. In 1959, Lucille Ball attempted to obtain the rights to this Rodgers and Hart musical as a potential special for her and Vivian Vance with the main male roles rewritten to feature the two actresses. Since the musical is basically a satire on gender roles, having Lucy and Vivian play the main roles intended for men would probably have meant changing all the female roles to males and vice versa, eliminating most of the satire.

Serial Queen

One solo possibility for Lucy suggested in the Desilu memo was to appear as the star of an action serial that was very popular with audiences in the early days of silent films. Apparently, no script was written for this special but speculation is that Lucy's character would have been an amalgam of the various heroines who starred in such presentations. For example, produced by Thomas Edison in 1912, *What Happened to Mary* featured Mary Fuller as a young woman who travels to New York City and becomes involved in a series of misadventures. The *Hazards of Helen* was another such early serial with Helen Holmes playing an employee of the railroad foiling train robberies, stopping runaway trains, and jumping off bridges. The most famous of the serials was *The Perils of Pauline* featuring Pearl White as a young woman who inherits a fortune when her guardian dies, but her late guardian's secretary attempts to keep the money by arranging various misfortunes to befall her.

Next Week, East Lynne

Published in 1950, this book written by actress/writer Gladys Hurlbut chronicled Hurlbut's early career as a stock company actress putting on plays in various small towns in the 1920s and 1930s. As she describes herself, "I was short and round and redheaded and very nearsighted."[43] However, she had fairly steady employment as a lead actress in a variety of theater presentations in towns and cities working for companies that would stay in one place for several weeks putting on a different play each week.

The book details the types of audiences, lead actors, character actors, and others that she experienced in her decade on the road. Hulburt left acting in the early 1930s to become a writer but returned to the stage in 1948 when she was fifty with a featured role in the sequel to *Life with Father* called *Life with Mother*. Thereafter, she continued to have small parts in movies and television from the 1950s until the early 1960s. She had a role in the Lucy and Desi feature film, *The Long, Long Trailer*.

Exactly how the book would have been adapted as a special for Lucy is not clear since Ms. Ball in 1960 was approximately the age of Hulburt when she made her comeback to the stage in 1948. One can speculate that maybe the TV special would have had Lucy playing Hulburt when she resumed acting with flashbacks to her earlier days. The flashbacks may have featured a younger actress or Lucy herself made up to look twenty-five years younger. Another alternative may have been to simply base the character Lucy would have played on one that had the same experiences as Ms. Hulburt but at an older age.

The book does contain several passages that would have been tailored to Ms. Ball's brand of physical comedy. For example, Hulburt played a vamp in a play, *Captain Applejack*, where she had to wear a black wig and red dress with a bolt of red sateen wrapped and pinned around her waist as a sheath. During many performances, the sheath would start unwinding with the consequence that she would have to twirl the other way around to get herself dressed again. There was also the time that the property manager gave her a real dagger instead of a blunt one, and she accidentally stabbed her leading man in the hand as she spiraled around in her red sateen. In a later performance, she fell and broke her arm and both her and her leading man who had been stabbed each played with their right arms in slings for weeks. Ms. Hulbert and her lead then had to perform in a new play where they had to perform "patty cakes" with the chorus with their arms in slings.

Ms. Hulburt also relates the time she drank too much champagne at a weekend party. She was initially pleased that she could carry her champagne so well until the Monday matinee. As she describes:

> I felt quite all right until my entrance but then the bright lights and my inevitable stage fright stirred up that champagne and when I romped on in my white riding breeches, slapping my crop against my boots, the stage rose and hit me in the face! Before I could slap it down, the floor turned into great rolls of cotton into which I sank whenever I took a step. My voice came from a different corner of the stage every time I spoke and the actors swayed before me in waves of vertigo.[44]

One can easily envisage how Lucy would have played such scenes.

Size 12

Written by Jerome Weidman in 1952, this never produced screenplay for RKO dealt with the fashion design business in New York City. The lead characters were Myra Doyle, a model who is in charge of all the models at the design firm, Gorgeous Gowns. In her late thirties and still a size 12, Myra never married and still lives with her parents. The owners of Gorgeous Gowns are Daisy and Rudy Roberts. Daisy, also in her late thirties, has devoted her life to creating dress designs, but major success in the industry has eluded her. Husband Rudy, her partner in the business, focuses on marketing the creations designed by his wife. Dan Stroud, the main salesman for the company, spends most of his time on the road selling the fashion line to various department stores.

If the script had been adapted as a TV special, presumably Lucille Ball would have had the role of Myra Doyle.

The plot centers on the company's disastrous summer fashion line which isn't selling and the efforts of the Roberts along with Myra to keep the company afloat to launch its fall line. It also deals with the roles of women pursuing a career in 1950s America – a common theme of many of these unproduced specials.

John Metcalf, a supplier of fabrics to the company, meets with the Roberts to ask when they will pay the outstanding bills owed to his company. He refuses to provide any more material to Gorgeous Gowns until the bills are paid threatening the launch of the fall line. Meanwhile, Daisy has hired a new model, eighteen-year-old Katie Carter, bypassing Myra in the hiring process which upsets her. Katie is interested in doing anything to get to the top of the modeling business. Daisy, jealous of her husband's interaction with Myra, wants to fire her and informs her husband to either get rid of Myra or offer her another position in the company. Afraid to terminate Myra, Rudy instead suggests that she take a long vacation which she questions given that the firm is about to launch its new line.

At home that night, Myra's mother surprises her with a birthday party whose guests include her co-workers and Dan Stroud who is in love with Myra and would like to marry her. At their apartment, Rudy and Daisy try to have dinner but argue about her role in the company. Rudy says that instead of trying to be a second-rate man in the firm, she should want to be a first-rate woman at home. Knowing that he needs to find money to pay off John Metcalf so Gorgeous Gowns can launch its new fashion line, Rudy phones Myra and asks her to meet with buyer B.L. Carroll, the head of a chain of department stores, to convince him to buy the summer line in order to pay off Metcalf. When Myra goes to Carroll's hotel room, he is not interested in seeing her. Learning from Myra that Carroll doesn't want to do business with Gorgeous Gowns, Rudy works out a deal with Nat Morgan, a bargain basement buyer, to purchase the existing inventory of summer dresses. Morgan then wants to have lunch with Myra, but she turns him down. Furious that her rejection might endanger the deal, Rudy argues with her, and Daisy joins in. Myra responds that Daisy got the company into financial difficulties with her disastrous summer line. Daisy in turn says that the dresses didn't sell because of how Myra was showing them. Myra quits.

She begins looking for another job as a model but, despite the fact that she is still a size 12, her age works against her. Dan visits her to say that the only bodies that remain a size 12 forever are those found in a wax museum. He later meets with Rudy and Daisy demanding that they give Myra her old job back or else he will quit.

The Roberts rehire Myra as they are about to show off their new line featuring a debutante collection of dresses for young women. Katie, the new model, informs Myra that the only reason she was rehired was because Dan forced the Roberts into taking her back. Myra confronts Daisy over this. Daisy says it is true and that, once the fall line showing is over, Myra will be finished with the firm. Myra decides to attempt to model one of the new fashions in front of the crowd watching the fashion show but ends up looking foolish in a dress designed for a much younger person. The audience begins to laugh at her as she exits the runway. Myra realizes that her modeling days are over, and she contemplates leaping into the freight elevator shaft. Dan saves her. At the end of the presentation, Daisy is left alone as Rudy and Katie go off together.

This would have been a rare dramatic turn for Lucy if she had starred as Myra Doyle in a television version of the screenplay.

Texas Guinan Project

"Texas" Guinan, born Mary Louise Cecilia in 1884, was an actress, movie producer, and business owner during the very early part of the twentieth century.

Guinan started out as a chorus girl in vaudeville and theater productions adopting the nickname "Texas" to make her stand out from other entertainment wannabes. She became a star vocalist in several Broadway musicals and lent her name to a weight-loss plan developed by W.C. Cunningham claiming that she had lost seventy pounds on the plan which was later revealed as a fraud.

Guinan next turned to making silent films in 1917 through the date of her death at forty-nine in 1933. She starred mostly in Westerns and was billed as "the female Bill Hart." She created her own production company, Texas Guinan Productions in 1921 and made three films. Guinan also became involved in the bootleg liquor business when Prohibition came into effect – putting on floor shows in speakeasy's and sharing in a percentage of the profits. She was arrested and indicted on charges of violating a law against "suggestive dances" but was later acquitted of the charges. Guinan contracted dysentery in Chicago and died on November 5, 1933.

Guinan was later portrayed in certain movies including 1945's *Incendiary Blonde* and 1961's *The George Raft Story*. Given her notoriety and variety of careers in the entertainment business, a dramatic teleplay based on her life would have been a fascinating vehicle for the talents of Lucille Ball playing someone other than her typical "Lucy" character.

Fancy Meeting You Again

George S. Kaufman and Leueen MacGrath wrote a play in 1951 about the idea of reincarnation. The play was considered as a possibility for a Lucy special with the redhead appearing as a sculptor named Amanda Phipps who is about to marry Martin Vellabrook. When the judge marrying the couple comes to the part of the vows about ". . . cleave only unto him, till death do ye part," Amanda backs out of the wedding. Twice before, Amanda had gotten cold feet about marrying a man. She confesses to her secretary that she has always been in love with a man who has had different names but whom she doesn't really know. She fantasizes about being in the Stone Age with a man called Gurd who bears a striking resemblance to Martin and another man. After the fantasy scene, Sinclair Heybore, an art critic, stops by to interview Amanda. He looks much like the other man in her Stone Age fantasy, and she blurts out that she is in love with him.

Heybore leaves on a lecture tour. Two weeks later, Amanda is asking about him. In the meantime, he has published a negative review of Amanda's latest work – a large nude woman, calling it a mass of clumsy stone. Amanda is convinced that Heybore is really the man for her that she has dreamed about in previous incarnations.

When Heybore visits Amanda again, he asks her to marry him. She says "yes." However, Martin warns Heybore about Amanda. She divulges that she has loved Heybore for thousands of years in all of her previous incarnations. Heybore's mother also believed in reincarnation which he says made his father's life miserable. Heybore confesses that he loves Amanda but doesn't want to marry her. Nevertheless, Amanda insists on marriage. A mysterious visitor tells Amanda that her soul is being called in. In fifteen separate lives, she has never gotten better than a "D" for conduct. She asks for one more chance to marry. Just in time, Heybore returns and asks again to marry Amanda.

This play would have been a departure from the usual character Lucille Ball portrayed on television. The work relied more on verbal humor than physical comedy. For example, in one scene talking about her past lives, Amanda says that when she was a slave girl, a man bought her for ten pieces of silver one day and sold her for twelve pieces the next day. Her secretary observes, "The next day! Say, you must have been lousy." To which Amanda replies, "No, he just couldn't resist a capital gain."[45]

Happy Birthday

A 1946 Broadway play called *Happy Birthday* by Anita Loos was also in the Desilu memo as a possible Lucille Ball vehicle. The play originally starred Helen Hayes in the role of Addie, a single, attractive librarian who visits a bar, the Jersey Mecca in Newark, New Jersey on a rainy night.

Addie Bemis has never been in a bar before despite or because of her father being a drunkard. She comes to the Jersey Mecca to meet a bank teller, Paul Bishop, with whom she has done business. Bishop enters the bar to see his girlfriend, Maude. Addie goes to their table to tell Paul that her father is after him because he has the idea that she is going to leave home for Paul. She had divulged to her dad that she frequently goes to the bank to see Mr. Bishop which upset her dad. Her father warned her that he will find Bishop and hurt him.

Paul invites Addie to sit at the table with Maude and him. Having never tasted liquor before, Addie orders ginger ale but then decides to try a Pink Lady. Paul and Maude discuss their wedding and honeymoon plans. Maude reveals, much to Paul's surprise, that when they go to California on their honeymoon, she may want to stay there instead of returning to Newark. Maude wants to get rid of Addie at the table. Paul decides to dance with Addie and, in the process, move her to another table. He successfully passes her off to a pair of old ladies and goes back to Maude. Addie talks with the elderly ladies while ordering a straight scotch. The drunker she becomes, the more she thinks of calling Maude's boss at a hair salon and invite him to come to the bar because, the gossip is that he is attracted to Maude. And so, Addie phones Maude's boss, Mr. Nanino.

Drunker than ever, Addie starts talking with others at the establishment including a woman named Myrtle who is there alone on her birthday since her boyfriend is with his wife. Addie decides to throw a party for Myrtle and buys champagne for everyone. She delivers a speech to the patrons wishing Myrtle "Happy Birthday" saying that anybody can have a birthday anytime they desire and that she feels born all over and wishes herself "Happy Birthday." Meanwhile, Mr. Nanino enters the bar and sits with Maude. Paul approaches their table and declares that Maude is with him. He subsequently learns that Maude may have been having an affair with her boss. After Maude tries to make up with Paul, she leaves the Jersey Mecca. Addie consoles the banker.

Addie's father, drunk as ever, comes to the bar looking for her. She and Paul hide under a table as Paul begins kissing her. They reveal themselves after Mr. Bemis sees them. He comes at Paul with a bottle, but Addie wrenches it from him and hits him over the head. After Maude phones the bar asking to speak with Paul, he leaves to see her. Bemis is proud that his daughter is no longer the staid old maid he thought she was.

Everyone begins leaving the establishment. The phone rings. It is Paul asking Addie for a date. He comes back to the Mecca having never gone to see Maude and walks toward Addie's table.

Happy Birthday was no doubt considered for Lucille Ball in the role of Addie Bemis because, among other situations, the main character, starting out with non-alcoholic beverages, becomes progressively drunker as the play goes on allowing Lucy to show her talent as she did, for example, in the first *Lucille Ball-Desi Arnaz Hour* with her character and Ann Sothern's character becoming drunk while in a Mexican jail cell.

"The Widow with the Serpent's Tongue"

From a book called *Forgotten Ladies* by Richardson Wright written in 1928, Desilu considered adapting one chapter about crusading journalist and widow Anne Royall as a solo possibility for Lucille Ball.

Anne Royall, born in 1769 who died in 1854, was married to plantation owner William Royall who passed away sixteen years after their marriage. Anne Royall began touring the Deep South and chronicling her impressions. After losing a court battle over inheriting her late husband's estate, she traveled to Washington to lobby Congress and other officials for a pension as the wife of a Revolutionary War veteran. To make ends meet, she came up with the idea of traveling around America observing the people and places and writing about her travels.

She published a book in 1826, *Sketches of History, Life and Manners in the United States* which caused something of a sensation because she called most people by their real names and, for those she didn't name, readers could usually figure out who they were. She wrote a total of ten such non-fiction books. Her works included observations like the women of Baltimore being the worst dressed, the prevalence of ignorance in Richmond, and describing the University of Pennsylvania as "a den of ignorance." She also had a low opinion of evangelical missionaries and the women who supported them. She opined that "All the differences I perceive in Washington since I wrote the Sketches is that the people eat more, drink more, dress more, cheat more, lie more, steal more, pray more, preach more, and are more ignorant and indigent."[46]

Royall would say that she liked to write books that people will read and there is nothing like throwing in a little spice. She often supported unpopular causes like battling those who wanted to establish a state religion and championing the Masons against anti-Mason sentiment. Royall was charged with being a "common scold," found guilty, and placed on probation for a year. Eventually she published her own newspaper in Washington called *Paul Pry* which included political editorials and political and local news and sought to expose public scandals. She fought for free non-denominational public schools, liberal immigration and tariff laws, state rights regarding slavery, and a free press.

A teleplay based on her career as a journalist would obviously have been dramatic allowing Lucille Ball to play a poor, hardworking, libertarian journalist – something clearly different from her usual television roles.

Fanny

"The Fanny Brice Story," before it became the hit musical and movie *Funny Girl*, was another Lucy special contemplated by Desilu. The initial screenplay was a proposed Hollywood bio-pic about Brice's show business accomplishments and her love affair with Nick Arnstein and ultimate divorce from him after he left prison for being convicted, in the screenplay, of accepting stolen bonds from two con men.

The screenplay contains several comic scenes such as one about Brice's first appearance in the Ziegfeld Follies. After singing a torch song with deep emotion and looking radiant, Fanny raises her gown to mid-calf height, revealing enormous naked pink rubber feet and clomps majestically off the stage. In another scene, lampooning Camille with Bert Lahr as Armand and W.C. Fields as a maid, a green spotlight appears on Fanny's face during the coughing scene with her body like a seal's and with her clapping her hands like flippers.

For a scene about Fanny's home life preparing dinner, the comedienne has two live carp swimming in her bathtub. While trying to kill one of the fishes with a wooden mallet, there is a knock on her apartment door. Nick Arnstein appears unexpectedly. With the fish in her hand, she hurries back to her bathroom, kicking the door shut. Placing the fish back in the tub, Fanny sniffs her fingers, winces, washes her hands quickly, and then, in the mirror – sees how disheveled she is. Scowling, she sits on the edge of the bathtub looking down at the fish. Looking disgusted and referring to the fish, she says "Move over!".

While Lucille Ball never appeared as Fanny Brice in this version of Brice's life, there was discussion that actress Judy Holiday would play the part. But instead, Ray Stark, Fanny Brice's son-in-law, decided to make the biography of his mother-in-law into a Broadway musical.

Sweet Jab in the Morning

Exactly what this play, written by Lucille S. Prumbs in 1958, is about is a mystery. Prumbs had previously written the plays, *Five Alarm Waltz* about an author and his playwright wife and *I'll Take the High Road* dealing with an American Fascist. Each had very brief runs on Broadway in the early 1940's.

Other than the characters being described as absurd and looney, the story line of *Sweet Jab in the Morning* is not known. Legendary theatrical and literary agent, Lucy Kroll, distributed copies of the work to various Broadway and TV producers in the late 1950's. Among the comments on the play is the following from Michael Ellis, "I wanted to stop at the end of the first ten pages but forced myself to finish the first scene. It compounded the felony to so do. I'm afraid the play is beyond me. I honestly couldn't make head or tale of it."[47]

Among the individuals to whom Kroll sent the play was Dorothy Hechtlinger of Desilu. In a letter to Ms. Kroll from Hechtlinger dated September 28, 1959, Ms. Hechtlinger writes, "... there was no enthusiasm for it (*Sweet Jab in the Morning*) and so I am returning it to you herewith." She goes on to state, "I am desperately in need of a solo starring vehicle for Lucille Ball for television. If there is anything you can recommend, by all means send it along."[48]

The "Almost" *I Love Lucy* Cast Reunion: "Lucy Goes to Broadway"

After Lucy divorced Desi, instead of continuing to appear on television specials or series, she decided to star in a movie with Bob Hope called *The Facts of Life* and tackle Broadway in a musical called *Wildcat*. The musical focused on Wildcat "Wildy" Jackson who dreams of striking oil but has neither the knowledge nor money to do so. Joe Dynamite (Keith Andes), a successful crew foreman, agrees to help her if she can show she owns the property on which she thinks there is oil and also hire a crew.

Desi Arnaz helped to finance the show and suggested to Madelyn Pugh Davis and Bob Carroll Jr. that they write a TV special called "Lucy Goes to Broadway" – a comic account of Lucy's television persona going to New York City for a part in a musical. Plans were to film the special during the day so as not to interfere with Lucy's evening performances in *Wildcat*.

Although divorced, Desi Arnaz showed up at the premiere of Wildcat *to congratulate his former wife on her Broadway debut.*

Although the special was never made, a script was written by Davis and Carroll, Jr. that would have starred Lucy, Vivian Vance, and William Frawley supposedly playing themselves but having the personalities of their *I Love Lucy* characters. Also, to be featured in the special were Bob Hope, Hedda Hopper, Michael Kidd and Richard Nash (the producers of *Wildcat*), Keith Andes, Leonard Bernstein, and Ed Sullivan.

Based on the first draft script, the special begins with Lucy arriving at Sardi's Restaurant after the opening night of *Wildcat*. Vivian Vance is in attendance, hugs Lucy, and then flashes back to what has transpired over the preceding six months.

Vivian is staying at a hotel in New York City when Lucy arrives at the same establishment. Lucy is in town for a few weeks and decides to move into Viv's hotel suite. Lucy begins complaining about how baggy her knit dress is only to be reminded that Viv is the one who made the dress for her. Viv informs Lucy that Bob Hope is staying in the same hotel to which Lucy responds that Hope is her "ex-buddy." She goes on the explain that during the flight to New York she was sitting in front of Hope, pushed her seat back while he was tying his shoe, and hit his nose. Later, the plane encountered some turbulence during which Lucy's big purse fell out of the overhead compartment and hit Hope's nose again.

Vivian remarks to Lucy that she might do the lead in a Broadway musical. Lucy receives a phone call to set up an appointment to audition for a musical also. Simultaneously, both blurt out that the musical is *Wildcat*. Each looks sick about the situation. Lucy says that they shouldn't compete against each other and that one of them should back out. Viv asks Lucy how she can do a musical when she can't sing. Furthermore, Viv says that Lucy won't be able to get the lead because Viv knows that Bob Hope is one of the show's backers.

Lucy thinks that she will apologize to Hope so he will put in a good word for her with producers, Michael Kidd and Richard Nash. However, Viv suggests that they both should decline to appear in the production. Lucy says she agrees but has her own ideas.

She decides to take flowers and champagne to Hope's room but sees Viv coming down the hall and so hides in another hallway beside a metal serving cart. A waiter moves the cart past Lucy. A loose loop of yarn from her knit dress catches on to a screw on the back of the cart. Her dress sleeve begins unraveling. She can't say anything because she will reveal herself to Vivian. She is unable to break the yarn because it is nylon. Both Viv and the waiter with the serving cart get into the elevator. As the elevator goes down, Lucy is almost jerked off her feet and runs toward the elevator door with her arm outstretched in front of her. Her dress begins unraveling around the neck. She is forced to keep turning around so as not to be pulled up against the elevator door. Each time the elevator stops at a floor, Lucy tries to bite the yarn with her teeth but to no avail. Spinning around so much, she begins to get dizzy. Lucy has the idea of trying to unwind the yarn herself to get ahead of things, but when the elevator starts again, she is pressed up against the elevator doors on her floor. Finally, the yarn breaks with Lucy sent spinning back across the hall and wearing only her slip.

She puts on another dress and goes to see Hope who has a bandage on his nose. He allows her to come into his room as he begins to eat lunch. Hope forgives Lucy for the nose injury, but when she opens the champagne, the cork hits his nose. She asks Hope to say to the *Wildcat* producers how great she would be as the lead in the musical. Hope claims that he is not a financial backer of the show. As she is ready to leave, Michael Kidd appears at Bob's hotel room door to apologize for the misleading article in *Variety* about the comedian investing in the show. Lucy uses the opportunity to say how great Michael Kidd is. Vivian then comes to the door with flowers and champagne for Bob. Initially she doesn't see Lucy and Kidd until Bob points them out. She questions what Lucy is doing there, and both of them tell Kidd that they want to speak with him about the lead in *Wildcat*. Michael says that Lucy would be perfect for the main role and explains to Viv that he is directing a revival of *Come Back, Little Sheba* and that she would be wonderful for the lead in that play. Kidd also advises Hope that he can still invest in *Wildcat*.

Time passes. Viv is memorizing her lines for *Come Back, Little Sheba*, while Lucy is rehearsing for *Wildcat* with a big bass drum. Lucy asks Viv to help her with the song from the musical, "Hey, Look Me Over." While rehearsing the number, the hotel manager phones saying that a man in the room below Lucy and Viv's, who is trying to nap, is complaining about the noise. There is a knock on their hotel room door. Who should be standing their wearing a night shirt, night cap, and old bathrobe but William Frawley – the grouch from downstairs? Frawley asks Lucy and Viv which one of them was holding a cat and which one was beating it with a baseball bat. They respond that they were simply rehearsing *Wildcat*. Frawley replies that he knew it wasn't *The Sound of Music*. He asks if Lucy is really doing a musical when she can't even sing. Frawley decides to leave and resume his nap.

Next, Bob Hope comes by and thinks someone in the room was hitting a drum with a sick cat. He is concerned about his recent investment in the musical. Lucy asks him to give her more time to rehearse. After Bob told gossip columnist Hedda Hopper about the new musical, she stops by to hear Lucy sing. Until her vocalizing improves, Lucy doesn't want to perform for Hopper. She pretends to have laryngitis. Viv handles the interview but talks mostly about her upcoming appearance in *Come Back Little Sheba*. Lucy begins pantomiming for Viv to go to the bedroom to rehearse. Bob picks up the interview talking about his upcoming projects. Lucy then attempts to respond to Hedda's questions by doing charades. She pantomimes that she used to be a Goldwyn Girl. When Hedda asks Bob if he has heard Lucy sing, he replies that she has a voice you wouldn't believe. Trying to impress Hopper, Lucy begins silently mouthing the words for "Hey, Look Me Over" and beating the drum at appropriate intervals. To which, Hedda responds that the song is marvelous and that she can hardly wait to hear it.

After Hedda departs, Vivian comes out of her bedroom to suggest that maybe Lucy could pantomime the entire musical. Lucy decides that she may need help with her singing and seeks to find someone to give her voice lessons. She phones Leonard Bernstein who tells her to come right over to Carnegie Hall. Bernstein asks the New York Philharmonic Orchestra to take a break, while he attempts to help Lucy. He begins playing "Hey, Look Me Over" on the piano. When Lucy sings, he says that it sounds like listening to a bagpipe. Bernstein advises Lucy that she is singing through her nose too much. He reaches over with his thumb and fore finger to pinch her nose shut. Lucy begins to sing better.

Lucy successfully lands the lead in *Wildcat* and starts rehearsals with her co-star Keith Andes. Keith and Lucy sing "Give a Little Whistle" with Lucy now having difficulty whistling. She becomes light-headed trying all sorts of ways to whistle but finally is successful. The following day, Lucy is trying the choreography for the production. She becomes exhausted from rehearsing and begins falling asleep. That night, she is to appear in the audience on *The Ed Sullivan Show*. When Ed introduces her and the cameras pan to her seat in the audience, Lucy is fast asleep. Viv, sitting next to her, holds Lucy's arm up like a prize fighter.

Opening night finally arrives with Bob Hope visiting a very nervous Lucy in her dressing room. He says there are no seats left in the audience having sold his two complimentary tickets to Bing Crosby. Michael Kidd and Richard Nash come by to wish Lucy luck. She confesses to Vivian that she is scared stiff and can't remember her opening number. Bob and

Viv try to reassure her, but it doesn't seem to work. Bob suggests that someone else will probably have to go on in Lucy's place and that someone should be Vivian. Lucy jumps to her feet and goes on stage. The play is a hit.

There was to be a tag at the end of the special. While it was not written, Davis and Carroll, Jr. mention in the script that Desi and/or Lucie Arnaz and Desi Arnaz Jr. may have appeared.

Filming of the special was canceled due to Ms. Ball's exhaustion from the requirements of appearing in *Wildcat*. The special was originally scheduled to air December 3, 1961 on CBS. The musical *Wildcat* ran for only 171 performances due to Lucy's exhaustion and illness from appearing every night in a Broadway show.

Lucy in Europe and Elsewhere

After renegotiating her contract with CBS for another season of *The Lucy Show*, Lucille Ball, who by now was president of Desilu, committed to three specials in addition to her comedy series.

Only one of the specials ever aired – "Lucy in London" on October 24, 1966 with Anthony Newley and the Dave Clark Five. Originally this special was to take place in Paris – not London, but evidently France would not permit filming a special there. After the negative critical reaction to "Lucy in London," the comic actress abandoned the other two.

One of the unproduced specials would have starred Lucy and Mitzi Gaynor as two nuns touring Europe with the Mitzi character having extra-sensory perception. The other special was titled "Lucy in Arabia." Perhaps for the latter, Lucille Ball sought to go back to the type of fantasy adventure she starred in with John Agar called *The Magic Carpet*. It was the last film she made before starting *I Love Lucy*.

As noted in Chapter 21, Lucille Ball planned at least one other special with Jackie Gleason that was never made.

Chapter 13: Other Desilu Unproduced Specials

In addition to the unproduced Lucille Ball specials, Desilu sought to make other types of specials which never came to fruition.

Don Quixote

In 1956, Desi Arnaz proposed a ninety-minute musical starring Dan Dailey as Don Quixote based on a screenplay written by Laszlo Vadnay. After airing it on television, Arnaz planned to release *Don Quixote* as a feature film.

When this proposal never materialized, in 1958, Arnaz thought of making *Don Quixote* an installment of *The Westinghouse Desilu Playhouse* with music by Johnny Green and Frank Loesser. Arnaz contemplated producing a total of six ninety-minute musicals with original books as part of *The Westinghouse Desilu Playhouse*, but none of these projects ever materialized. However, the anthology did air one original sixty-minute musical as its second season premiere in September 1959. "A Diamond for Carla," starring Anna Marie Alberghetti, focused on an orphan girl with no dowry whose foster mother wants her to marry a backward chap nicknamed Fishhead, but a wealthy yachtsman leaves Carla a diamond ring for her dowry freeing up her marriage choices.

The Industrialists

Desilu considered a series of ninety-minute specials profiling famous entrepreneurs such as Henry Ford. George Murphy was appointed liaison for the series to be made by Mort Briskin. Reynolds Metals, U.S. Steel, and Firestone Tire and Rubber were among the corporations approached about this 1960 project. Desi planned to meet with NBC about airing the specials after five or six firm deals on the personalities to be featured were made, but, again, nothing came of this project.

Chapter 14: Lucy's Unsold Funny Lady Comedy Pilots

While Desilu produced several half-hour comedy pilots under Lucille Ball's presidency, only one of them resulted in a series – *Glynis* starring Glynis Johns. *Glynis*, created by *I Love Lucy's* Jess Oppenheimer, dealt with a couple – Glynis Granville, a scatterbrained mystery writer and her attorney husband Keith (Keith Andes), who became involved in criminal cases as amateur sleuths. The series, originally called *Careful, My Love*, lasted only for half a season on CBS in fall 1963.

In a newspaper article titled "'Glynis' Seen as Combination of 'Lucy' and the 'Thin Man,'" which succinctly describes the concept of the series, Jess Oppenheimer felt that he had another *I Love Lucy* in *Glynis*. He remarked that ". . . Glynis is one of these rare people with great personal dignity who can run the gamut of emotions from drama to comedy."[49]

Reviewing the premiere of *Glynis*, *Variety* opined, "Served up was a rather creaky vehicle to launch Glynis Johns on a TV career that doesn't promise longevity unless what is billed as a situation mystery-comedy gives with more comedy which Miss Johns could fulfill admirably. Maybe she is not another Lucille Ball which may have been Jess Oppenheimer's first thought, but she is a fairly reasonable facsimile."[50]

It is ironic that Lucille Ball, the "Queen of Comedy," had such poor luck with comedy pilots but was behind the sale of three iconic dramatic series – *Star Trek*, *Mission: Impossible*, and *Mannix* to the networks.

Oscar Katz, whom Lucy hired to run the production company, employed several writer/producers to develop pilots. Among the hires were the team of Hal Goldman and Larry Klein to create three new comedies, Martin Jurow, former president of Famous Artists to produce three pilots, and Gene Roddenberry to develop new one-hour dramatic series.

Writer/producer Jess Oppenheimer who, after producing I Love Lucy, *created other Lucy-like comedies such as* Angel, The Debbie Reynolds Show, *and* Glynis.)

Many of the following unsold comedy pilots aired on *Vacation Playhouse* under a deal Desilu had with CBS to broadcast its pilots as a summer replacement for *The Lucy Show*.

Maggie Brown

Ethel Merman and Susan Watson doing a number in Maggie Brown.

This Ethel Merman sitcom attempt began development in 1962 while Desi was still the head of the studio. Projected for the 1963-64 television season, the comedy was initially called *The Ethel Merman Show* and then *Trader Brown*.

In the 1963 pilot, Merman played the title character – the larger-than-life owner of a bar on tropical Lobster Island that housed a Navy base with 1200 sailors. Commander John Farragut (Roy Roberts) headed the base. Maggie lived there with her teenage daughter Jeannie (Susan Watson) and her bartender/piano player.

At the beginning of the pilot, Maggie sings "Friendship" to the sailors in her bar. McChesney (Walter Burke), the owner of a competing bar, complains to Farragut that Maggie is making illegal beer which indeed she is in order to raise money to send her daughter to a private school in Connecticut.

However, her beer-making machine, located in the basement, is broken, and the sailor that used to fix it has been transferred. Her brew master, Marv (Marvin Kaplan) finds another sailor named Joe Beckett (Mark Goddard), a machinist, who can repair the machine, but Joe demands 50% of her profits. He accepts 25% after he sees Maggie's cute daughter. To fix the equipment, Joe steals McChesney's bagpipes, the sounds from which are a dead giveaway to where the machine is located when the Commander and McChesney make a surprise visit to Maggie's place. The Commander places Maggie's bar off-limits to his sailors. Learning of this, every patron of the bar pays their IOU's to raise the money so Maggie's daughter can attend school. But Maggie changes her mind and decides not to send Jeannie away. Mother and daughter sing "Mutual Admiration Society," and the bar is re-opened.

Cy Howard and Arthur Julian created the concept for the pilot. Bill Manhoff wrote the script; and David Alexander directed it. This pilot was the first one to be shot in color by Desilu. In discussing the project, Merman said "There's nothing like it on TV now. It's a half-hour that's partly situation comedy and partly musical comedy. I'll be able to sing two songs each week."[51] Despite lobbying from Lucille Ball for the pilot to become a series, no network picked it up. ABC came the closest to turning it into a series even thinking of scheduling it at 9:30 pm on Fridays for the 1963-64 season but ultimately decided to schedule *The Farmer's Daughter* with Inger Stevens in that time slot.

Working Girls

This 1963 comedy project concerned four young woman, all sharing the same apartment, who have to work for a living. Tuesday Weld was to be one of the stars. Evidently, no pilot was ever filmed.

According to news reports at the time, producer Martin Jurow had been working on a situation comedy called *Working Girl* with almost the same premise as the Weld project. Jurow threatened legal action if Desilu went ahead with the Tuesday Weld series.[52]

A-Okay O'Shea

Like *Maggie Brown*, this planned 1963 project started development under Desi Arnaz's presidency. It was designed for the talents of Gale Storm who had starred on two successful sitcoms, *My Little Margie* and *Oh! Susanna*.

In the pilot script for *A-Okay O'Shea*, written by Lee Karson and Ray Allen, Storm starred as Captain Daphne O'Shea, an Assistant Special Services Officer at a base, Fort Klondike, in Alaska. She reported to Major Bruce Wingfield, the Chief of Special Services who is convinced that his specialty of athletics and recreation is the backbone of military life. O'Shea had two assistants, Staff Sergeant Irving Oomiak, a young Eskimo and head of the Recreation Section, and Sergeant Cabot Caldwell, a young non-com head of the Athletic Section. Corporal Edna Trimble was a plain-looking clerk-typist in the Special Services Office.

"Vocal Boy Makes Good," the pilot's title, dealt with rock 'n roll singer Bobby Tyler being inducted into the Army and sent to Fort Klondike. At the other bases to which he had been assigned, his teenage followers created problems congregating outside the bases. O'Shea thinks having Tyler assigned to Fort Klondike will help raise morale at the base. However, upon arrival, Bobby, who considers himself the world's greatest singer, doesn't want to sing thinking the cold will damage his vocal cords. The men start complaining that, at the PX, the waitresses are always paying attention to Tyler and not waiting on them. Also, the singer has special food sent in by his agent and does not share it with others. After Daphne berates Bobby for his behavior, he seeks to square himself with the other guys on the base. Not knowing this, Major Wingfield volunteers Tyler for a unit headed by Major Barnes involving driving trucks along with various maintenance duties. When O'Shea finds out, she wants him back now that Tyler has apologized. She uses a dog sled to go after him.

The pilot involved plenty of slapstick like O'Shea inadvertently getting involved with a group of men practicing acrobatics and ending up in the rafters of a building, mistakenly drinking a chemical designed to break the enemies will to fight and becoming complacent to the Major's comments, and wearing battery-heated underwear that begins to smoke and melt snow.

Citing the fact that "the elements weren't right," this project was shelved by Desilu in February 1963 before a pilot was ever filmed.[53]

Exclusively Connie

Actress Jane Powell, working with writer Robert Blees, wanted to make a pilot in 1964 variously titled *Cyn's for Me* or *Exclusively Connie* to be produced by Desilu. At the time, Oscar Katz was not particularly fond of the project, and apparently nothing came of this endeavor.

The Lady Is a Champ

In mid-1964, Desilu and CBS explored developing a new sitcom for the mercurial Betty Hutton. Ed Jurist and Alexander Rose did a pilot script for the proposed series, but no pilot came out of it.

The August 20, 1964 script has Hutton playing a housewife and community-activist named Pam Barton married to husband Pete, an advertising executive. They have a fourteen-year-old daughter named Immy.

Pam, a member of a group attempting to build a new playground in the town, is asked to convince wealthy J.J. Hirt not to renege on his pledge of $10,000 to purchase land for the project. Hirt is getting married in a few days and wants to redecorate his house. He is expecting a decorator to stop by to discuss the improvements. Whom should he mistake for the decorator but Pam? While he is out of the living room, Pam, in a scene right out of a Lucy comedy, attempts to pull open the draperies resulting in a situation with a falling ladder, a St. Bernard, and Pam ending up on the floor covered by the drapes.

Hirt leaves for the office without talking to Pam about his pledge. At work, Hirt learns that a former girlfriend of his wants money or she will sue for alienation of affection. Still pretending to be the interior decorator, Pam visits his office. Upon meeting Hirt, she confesses that she is not really the decorator. Thinking Pam is representing his former girlfriend, Hirt has her removed. She goes to her husband's place of work wanting to make a sign protesting Hirt's unfairness. From Pam, Pete learns that Hirt is looking for a new slogan for an advertising campaign. Pete and his partner Joe attempt to see Hirt to propose a new ad campaign. However, because Hirt is worried that his former love interest is having a subpoena issued for him, he hastily departs for his new construction site not having time to meet with Pete and Joe.

Pam is still pursuing him. Not knowing about Hirt's pending legal problems with his ex-girlfriend, a process server gives Pam the subpoena to deliver to Hirt. To get to him, Pam has to ascend to the fourteenth floor of the skeletal structure on his construction site. Perched on a girder swinging from a crane, she presents Hirt with a paper in her pocket which turns out not to be the subpoena but notes she was given by her husband on how to approach Hirt about his pledge. Upon reading the paper, Hirt believes the note is a slogan for his new ad campaign – "if you want a happy home, you've got to have heart." He reads "heart" as "Hirt." Pam gives credit for the slogan to her husband and then has Hirt renew his pledge for the playground.

This potential pilot was not the first time Betty Hutton sought to portray a character similar to Lucy Ricardo. The actress made a pilot in 1957 for Jess Oppenheimer's production company, Burlingame Productions. The pilot, initially titled *Hey Mom* and then *That's My Mom*, starred Hutton as a widow with four kids living in a rented house, part of Magnolia Mansions, managed by Mr. Tuttle (Herbert Anderson) on behalf of his Aunt Emmy Mae Mosley (Nina Varela) who was originally from South Carolina. The building complex prohibited children and pets from occupying any of the houses, but, in a moment of weakness, Tuttle had permitted Betty Beeman (Hutton) and her children – Judy (Nancy Randall), Jerry (Steve Stevens), Donny (John Moss), and Bobby (Donnie Baker) to move in.

When Aunt Emmy pays a surprise visit, Betty has to hurriedly clean up the living room to eliminate any signs of children and pets, which includes her character eating dog biscuits pretending they are a health food. However, Aunt Emmy soon finds the kids and the dog and orders the family to move out.

Betty comes up with a scheme, worthy of Lucy, to impersonate a woman named Betty Lou Mason-Dixon from the South, thinking that she can endear herself to the aunt. Using hot water bottles for padding on her behind and assuming a Southern accent, she convinces Aunt Emmy, after telling her that all of Betty's children have Southern names, to give her a lease allowing children and pets on the premises. In the process, naturally, Betty sits on the aunt's needle point piercing the hot water bottles with the expected results. Aunt Emmy soon finds out about Betty's impersonation and takes the lease from her. The children's dog then retrieves the lease from the aunt so Betty and her kids can stay in their house.

Roland Kibbee scripted the pilot which had a lot of physical comedy performed by Hutton and had the actress singing a couple of songs including "You're Nothing but a Hound Dog" and "Carolina in the Morning." Intended for the 1957-58 TV season on NBC, the pilot, directed by Robert Sidney, never sold.

Mother Is the Law (aka Mrs. Keystone and the Kops)

Another actress for whom Desilu attempted to design a comedy series was Jean Arthur. Hal Goodman and Larry Klein wrote the pilot script for the planned show. Desilu approached CBS about the project, but that network showed no interest.

The script focused on Maggie Taylor, a widowed mother of a fifteen-year-old daughter named Susie, who is a policewoman. Also, in the household is Pops Walker, Susie's grandfather. Susie complains that boys avoid her because her mother is a cop. She would like to throw a party at home but doesn't want her mother to chaperone. Pops plots to get Maggie out of the house on the night of the party by encouraging her to go on a date with Lieutenant Barney Simmons, her colleague at work. However, Maggie intercepts a phone call from the caterer for the party about an order for hamburgers and ice cream. She breaks her date with Barney in order to crash the party by disguising herself as the food delivery person. Seeing nothing untoward when she enters her house with the food, Maggie decides to leave, but still not feeling comfortable about her daughter's party, she spies through the windows in the back of her house. The next door neighbor thinks Maggie is a prowler and calls Susie to report what she is seeing. When the boys attending the party rush out of the house to catch the prowler, Maggie flees. After the party, Pops and Susie agree that they made a mistake by keeping the party a secret from Maggie.

A few years after this project, CBS did pick up *The Jean Arthur Show* in which Ms. Arthur starred as an attorney with her son played by Ron Harper. The series lasted for only half a season.

The Pearls

In fall 1964, Desilu contemplated a pilot about an exotic real estate woman who sells large tracts of land. Created by Martin Jurow with a script by Dorothy Cooper, the planned series was based on the exploits of an actual person who lived in Arizona.

My Lucky Penny

Created by Cy Howard and developed by Arnie Sultan and Marvin Worth, this comedy pilot starred Brenda Vaccaro as Jenny Penny married to aspiring dental student Ted (Richard Benjamin). Their friends are a married couple played by Luana Anders as Sybil Rockefeller and Joel Grey as Freddy Rockefeller. The Grey character was also a student studying to become a dentist.

The concept was that the wives had to work to support their husbands while they completed their education. Ted, in particular, didn't like his wife working. He and Freddy attempt to come up with money-making ideas of their own. Jenny works for the "Commodore" who is never seen but sounds very much like Cary Grant. The Commodore provides Jenny's assignments by audio tape which self-destructs as it is played. From experience, Jenny has found that things work out better when she doesn't follow her boss' instructions completely.

In the 1965 pilot, Jenny's new assignment from the Commodore is to pick up a package containing $16,000 in one dollar bills, put it in the Commodore's safe before turning it over to two men as payment from her boss. Jenny has problems transcribing the instructions including the combination to the safe because her typewriter is on a table that keeps revolving. She ends up taking the money home for safe-keeping. Sybil and Jenny try to hide the cash in a hole in the ground, but a dog digs it up. Ted and Freddy then decide to turn all the dollar bills into coins because the coins are too heavy for someone to steal. They put the coins in a locker at the bus station. Of course, Ted loses the key to the locker and believes that Freddy stole it. Sybil finds the key in the lining of Ted's jacket having fallen through a hole in his pocket. Ted and Freddy are unable to exchange the coins for dollar bills in time for the scheduled delivery of the cash, and so they pour the change down the chimney of its recipients. The Commodore is pleased with the outcome that the recipients will have to count every coin. Originally, he just wanted them to count the individual one dollar bills because he did not entirely believe that he owed them the $16,000.

The pilot went through several title changes before settling on *My Lucky Penny*. It was first called *Girl in the Window*, then *The Breadwinners*, and then *Jenny Penny*.

Chapter 15: Lucy's Unsold Funny Men Comedy Pilots

While Lucille Ball was head of Desilu, her chief in charge of production, Oscar Katz, commissioned several unsold pilots with males as main characters.

Hey, Teacher

This 1963 comedy pilot starred Dwayne Hickman of Dobie Gillis fame as a third-grade elementary school teacher named Joe Hannan.

Produced by Bob Sweeny and written by Hannibal Coons and Harry Winkler, the project had various titles during its development – *Never Tease a Dinosaur*, *Mr. Hannan and the Little People*, and *Never Trust a Dinosaur*. Both CBS and ABC rejected the proposed comedy.

The pilot dealt with Mr. Hannan's first day at the school as a new teacher fresh out of college finding that he is surrounded by female teachers and that the smartest man at the school is the janitor.

In his autobiography, Hickman relates a meeting he had with Lucille Ball about the pilot writing that she was all business and didn't want the show to be "Dobie Gillis Teaches School."[54] He also mentions that director Bob Sweeney didn't like the *Dobie Gillis* series. According to Hickman, he thinks this was because Sweeney's *Fibber McKee and Molly* comedy on which he played Fibber had been up against *Dobie Gillis* which beat it in the ratings causing NBC to cancel Sweeney's show after thirteen weeks.

The Hoofer

Based on a book by Jack Donohue chronicling his years as a dancer, this comedy was initially titled *Letters of a Hoofer to His Ma* before being shortened to *The Hoofer*. Donohue directed several episodes of *The Lucy Show* and *Here's Lucy* as well as this pilot.

Donohue's 1931 book included his letters to his mother detailing his performances in New England in the 1910's and his mother's replies to his correspondence. A June 14, 1910 letter, for example, reports a rather embarrassing experience Donohue encountered in Lewiston, Maine.

> I was watching this Fleurette that opens the bill. And while I was standing there in the wings, she smiled at me. She looked like a nice, sociable little dame and I figured I ought to give her a little encouragement because after all she was out there doing her best, so I smiled back at her and when she came off I gave her hand a little squeeze and asked her if she'd like a little coffee after the show. She said it was okay, real quick, and then ran back to take a bow. And then she pulls off her wig and it's a man all the time. Well, nobody else saw it and he didn't get sore, so I took him over for some coffee anyway.[55]

The 1963 pilot, set in the 1920s, starred Donald O'Connor as Donald Dugan, a vaudeville dancer and Soupy Sales as Fred Brady, his piano accompanist. The pilot had a lot of old jokes and wacky, physical humor.

The script, written by Ed Jurist and Bud Nye, opened with Brady participating in a poker game with two guys – Finnegan (Jackie Coogan) and Wake (Cliff Norton), their last names being a play on the title of the James Joyce novel, *Finnegan's Wake*. Brady thinks that the two are novices to the game but soon finds out that they conned him into participating and win all of his money.

After learning that a heavyweight bout will be broadcast on radio on a delayed basis, Dugan has an idea for recovering his money. He begins playing poker with Finnegan and Wake, while Brady turns on the radio to the delayed broadcast already knowing who won the fight. Donald bets $500 on the boxer who won with Finnegan and Wake betting on his opponent. Naturally, Dugan wins. After he leaves with the winnings, Finnegan and Wake hear that the fight was a rebroadcast.

The two vaudevillians then travel to Chicago to attempt to see booking agent, Brainsley Gordon (Jerome Cowan) to audition for his new revue. At their hotel, Dugan crashes a luncheon for a charitable association hoping to raise funds for a children's wing on a local hospital. He promises a special performance for the hospitalized children as his contribution to the association. Turning into the hospital's parking lot, the vaudevillians encounter Finnegan and Wake looking to get back their money. Dugan and Brady attempt to elude the gamblers with Donald placing a Boston Bag on his stomach, pretending to be a pregnant woman. After escaping from Finnegan and Wake, Brady and Dugan perform in a gymnasium with Brainsley Gordon in attendance. They execute a big slapstick acrobatic finale as the two gamblers try to catch them again.

CBS rejected the pilot. It was then shopped to NBC and ABC which also passed on it.

Papa G.I.

Made in late 1963, this project starred Dan Dailey as a former G.I. who adopts two Korean children and brings them to the United States. Jess Oppenheimer and Jameson Brewer wrote the script with Oppenheimer and Ed Feldman producing.

The pilot script opens with Sgt. Mike Harper (Dailey) finding Le Quang Duc and his sister, Le Kim Chi, along a road in Korea. Knowing that Mike puts on Army shows, the siblings entertain him with a vaudeville act. He hires them to help him with props and things for his shows. Subsequently, Mike receives orders to transfer back to the States. He is reluctant to tell Quang Duc and Kim Chi that he has to leave them. Because they want to go with Mike, they try to find prospective wives for him to marry so he can adopt them. When that scheme doesn't work out, they steal items from Mike's fellow G.I.'s thinking that he will have to stay in Korea to receive punishment unaware that he would land in jail. After Mike is arrested, his commanding officer releases him upon hearing Mike's version of events. Mike yells at Kim Chi and Quang Duc concerning their latest scheme, and the kids disappear. When the other guys in Mike's unit hold a farewell party for him, the siblings reappear to entertain. Touched by their act, Mike pledges that he won't leave Korea without them.

Originally titled *Papa San*, the pilot was considered by CBS, but the network rejected it.

My Uncle Louie

Billed as a "hootenanny-comedy," this was another effort by Cy Howard to come up with a comedy for Desilu. Howard had helped to launch three comedy series for the company – *Guestward Ho!, Harrigan and Son,* and *Fair Exchange,* none of which went beyond a single season, as well as several pilots as described in this book.

Just what the premise of a "hootenanny comedy" was is not clear. One can speculate that perhaps Uncle Louie ran a club where folk singers performed and the "My" in the title referred to a niece or nephew who appeared at the club. The project was launched in September 1963 but abandoned soon thereafter because of a stalemate in casting.

The Farmer from Palermo

Tonio Fiore was the farmer from Palermo in this mid-1964 comedy project written by Max Wilk. Tonio immigrated to the United States at the request of his uncle, Angelo. Several years earlier, Angelo had come to America with the help of Tonio's father where he founded his own construction company and prospered. Now he is hoping that his nephew will become a part of his company. However, Tonio is more interested in farming than in construction. When his uncle instructs him to select one of his vacant lots for his agricultural pursuits, Tonio, much to his uncle's dismay who had thought Tonio would have selected farm land in Connecticut or New Jersey, ends up choosing a valuable lot in New York City.

While Tonio agrees to take night courses in engineering and architecture, by day, he tills the soil on his uncle's vacant lot and raises vegetables and fruits. To circumvent city regulations, Tonio establishes the Fiore Agricultural Academy to open his gardens to visitors with profits from the sale of his produce going to maintain the land. The essential conflict on the proposed comedy was one between Uncle Angelo wanting to build an office building on the land and Tonio continuing to farm the area.

In the treatment written by Wilk, several possible story lines for episodes were outlined. When local produce markets recognize the impact Tonio's farm is having on their business, they want him to use a middle man in selling to customers. After Tonio refuses, the produce vendors plot to sabotage Tonio's crops but back off the idea and begin doing business with Tonio when a drought in the West causes a scarcity of fruits and vegetables. Another episode idea involved Angelo trying to marry off Tonio so he becomes less interested in farming. Angelo's housekeeper sends for her niece's daughter as a marriage prospect, but the girl ends up becoming a model and creating a substantial dowry to return to Italy to marry her boyfriend. A third story idea had Angelo having his friend, a real estate developer, speak with Tonio to move his farm to a less valuable piece of land but to no avail.

Evidently, no pilot was ever made for this proposed comedy.

My Son, The Doctor

Starring Kay Medford as Jenny Piper and Jeff Davis as her son, Dr. Peter Piper, this pilot, written by Hal Goodman and Larry Klein, concerned a young, married Westwood, California pediatrician whose mother serves as his office nurse. She believes that she knows more about kids than he does. The doctor shares his waiting room with bachelor, Walter Mayberry (Dick Patterson), a children's dentist. Peter, whose wife's name is Barbara, has two children. Patsy Kelly played Dr. Mayberry's nurse, Miss Primrose. Other characters in the pilot included Phil Sawyer, a medical supply salesman always trying to sell Dr. Piper items that he doesn't really need like chocolate covered tongue depressors and lollipops containing penicillin and Morton Gilmore, the local pharmacist.

The pilot, made in 1964, involves Dr. Piper's wife worrying that her husband has no time to enjoy life, and so she plans a surprise party for him. She plots to have the mother of one of his patients phone him at night to make an emergency house call and so have the party at the mother's house. Peter overhears his mother talking with Miss Primrose about the surprise party. Assuming it is at his house, he asks Dr. Hopkins to take his afterhours emergency calls. Dr. Hopkins ends up at the party with Dr. Piper arriving home to an empty house. When Barbara calls him, he thinks that she has left him, but she asks her husband to come to the party. After he arrives, Dr. Hopkins, who has been imbibing plenty of food, becomes ill, and Dr. Piper has to take his own emergency house calls.

In addition to the pilot script, Goodman and Klein laid out several story lines for additional episodes. A man calls Piper's office asking for medical advice but refuses to bring in the patient who turns out to be a chimpanzee. A second story line involved a family of thirteen seeing Dr. Mayberry for a dental checkup which they won on a show sponsored by a toothpaste company. Jenny talks the parents into a package deal to have the kids examined by her son Peter. After examining the entire brood, Dr. Piper finds out that they are visitors from Florida. Another plot had Jenny talking Dr. Mayberry into taking her son to the country club to find a more upscale clientele for his practice. Unable to socialize for financial gain, Dr. Piper claims to be a lawyer ending up with six lucrative law cases.

The Recruiters

Garry Marshall, creator of series like *Happy Days*, and his then writing partner Jerry Belson wrote the pilot for this military-themed comedy starring Dick Patterson, Bruce Hyde, and Elliott Reid as recruiters representing different branches of the Armed Forces.

Speaking to columnist Earl Wilson about the CBS pilot targeted for the 1966-67 TV season, Dick Patterson indicated, "It's a very funny show, but I'm just afraid that with the Viet Nam situation and the draft-card burners, military recruiting may be a touchy subject for a while."[56]

His Highness and O'Hara

This comedy attempt involved a female Irish schoolteacher and modern-day Gypsies. Written by Mike Morris and Larry Markes, they reported to columnist Hal Humphrey, "Remember we told you that we had a date at Desilu the day the car ran over me? Well, we thought it was to sign a deal for our pilot, His Highness and O'Hara . . . But suddenly Lucille Ball changed her mind and decided comedies won't be so big next season, so she wants Desilu to do adventure series instead."[57]

Chapter 16: Lucy's Unsold Parody and Fantasy Comedy Pilots

Under Lucille Ball's presidency, Desilu expanded its comedy projects to more than just ones focused on a male or female central character or funny couples. The studio entered the field of comedy parodies and fantasies without much luck.

The Unteachables

In late 1962, Cy Howard and Desilu attempted to develop for ABC a comedy set in the 1920's. It was shelved by November 1962. But about nine months later in June 1963, Howard resurrected the concept this time described as a "crime comedy" or more specifically, a comedy version of Desilu's hit series *The Untouchables*. Ed Jurist and Bud Nye were hired to write the pilot script called "Joe Sent Me" with Jonathan Winters considered as one of the leads. By November 1963, the project was abandoned again.

The pilot script focused on two bumbling police officers – Roland "Roley" Whipple who was married to Captain Flannagan's daughter and Pete Petersen described as Don Quixote in blue. Martin Trask, head of the Investigative Unit of the Division of Internal Revenue, learns that a council meeting of top mobsters will take place in the 12th Precinct where Flannagan is in charge. Figuring that the local mobster hosting the meeting, Big Nick Lombardi, will be entertaining some early arrivals at his Club Flamingo, Trask enlists men from the precinct to help with a raid on the club. Roley and Pete are two officers assigned to make sure no one escapes through the back of the club during the raid. As the raid is occurring, club members do run to the rear of the building with Pete holding a fire hose to douse them with water. However, Roley, who is supposed to turn on the fire hydrant, is distracted, and the members escape. Roley and Pete are suspended from the force for a week.

The two decide to leave the city for a vacation during their suspension. At the railroad station, they see Joe "the Gent" Schneider arrive for the syndicate meeting and try to arrest him for carrying a concealed weapon, but Joe flees. He boards a cattle car and escapes. Meanwhile, the driver who is supposed to pick up Joe for the meeting thinks that Pete is Joe because he has Joe's passport. The driver takes both Pete and Roley to the council meeting where the two officers hope to arrest the mobsters thereby getting in good graces with Capt. Flannagan. Shortly after arriving at the place, Nick Lombardi discovers that Pete and Roley are really police officers, but the two are able to escape and go to the precinct. There they learn that Trask had bugged the meeting place hoping to get the "goods" on the mobsters. Trask realizes that two police officers broke up the meeting before sufficient evidence could be obtained but the recording stops before the identities of the officers could be determined saving Pete and Roley's careers.

I Married a Martian

Shades of *Bewitched*, this comedy project was initially to star Julie Newmar and Jack Kelly (he of *Maverick* fame) in a tale about a Madison Avenue advertising executive who meets and then marries an attractive female who later reveals that she is a Martian living on Earth. When Kelly couldn't be signed for the pilot, Bob Cummings got the role of the ad executive. However, as with *A O'Kay O'Shea*, when Lucy assumed the presidency of Desilu, the project was shelved. Apparently concerned that other properties about Martians were under consideration by CBS for the 1963-64 season, Lucy canceled the filming of the pilot.

CBS did pick up a Martian comedy for the 1963-64 season, *My Favorite Martian*, produced by Jack Chertok. Ironically, in 1964, Chertok paired Newmar and Cummings in a comedy called *My Living Doll* where Newmar played a female robot who was cared for by psychiatrist Robert MacDonald (Bob Cummings).

I Married a Martian was created by Lee Karson and originally developed before Desi resigned as head of Desilu.

Hooray for Hollywood

Another Desilu comedy pilot set in the 1920s, *Hooray for Hollywood* was a project for CBS shot in late 1963 and aired on June 22, 1964. The pilot centered on the experiences of Jerome P. Baggley (Herschel Bernardi) who headed World Goliath Studios. Joan Blondell played Baggley's secretary, Miss Zilke, his ever-loyal servant who also narrated the show. The co-stars included Marvin Kaplan as Munroe, Baggley's brother-in-law and lackey, and Joyce Jameson as Vonda Renee, the studio's biggest star.

The story line dealt with Baggley's competitor, Leviathan Pictures, learning that Vonda's contract would expire soon and wanting to entice her away from Goliath Studios for $1 million. When Baggley realizes this, he offers her a $3 million movie about Marie Antoinette. However, when the bankers that support the studio find out about the money involved, they threaten to fire Baggley. After he informs them that the new contract Vonda signed is with him personally and not with the studio, they beg him to stay.

Produced by Warren Lewis, the test show was directed by Barry Shear based on a script by Sheldon Keller. It was a joint production of Desilu and Don Sharpe Productions.

Vacation with Pay

Shades of *Hogan's Heroes*, Desilu attempted to develop, in mid-1964, a comedy, set during World War II, about American G.I.'s incarcerated in a German border camp. The book, *Vacation with Pay: Being an Account of My Stay at the German Rest Camp for Tired Allied Airman at Beautiful Barth on the Baltic* by Alan H. Newcomb, served as the basis for the project.

Robert Blees wrote the script. An early draft of the script, titled *The POW's*, is set in 1944 Austria at Husselgupf Castle which the Germans have turned into a POW camp for captured American flyers. Oskar Hauptmann, age sixty, is the camp's commandant, having been conscripted by the Germans to run the camp because all the other able-bodied men in the local town are fighting the Allies. The prisoners in the camp are either plotting escapes or concealing items such as maps and a radio. When the camp's officers do their periodic shakedowns, the POW's have to quickly hide parts from the radio so they are not discovered.

Oskar asks Colonel Daye, the senior POW, to recruit a crew for a work project. The Americans are curious about the endeavor suspecting it is military-related. A group of the POW's volunteers for the work hoping to slow down progress on the project and to find out what it is about. They find that the Germans are building an airstrip for fighter planes. The POW's are able to transmit a message to the underground about the new landing strip. Allied planes then come to bomb its location.

ABC was interested in the proposal but apparently no pilot was made.

The Good Old Days

NBC considered this mid-1964 project by Hal Goodman and Larry Klein, a parody on *The Flintstones*, which itself was a take-off on *The Honeymooners*. Darryl Hickman and Bruce Yarnell starred as two cavemen. Howard Morris directed the pilot which was rejected by NBC in February 1965.

The first draft of the pilot script dated August 7, 1964 concerned Rok, a young caveman living with his parents – Mommy and Daddy and his young brother Kid. The family pet, a baby mastodon, was named Long Nose.

Rok decides to move out on his own even though his parents don't want him to leave. Trying to find his own cave, he encounters an unattractive woman named Ugh who offers him the opportunity to move in with her, but Rok declines the offer. Next Rok visits his best friend Kook, the local inventor, to ask him for advice. Kook suggests that Rok stay with a friend until he finds his own cave. Kook advises him to move in with Slag, the most powerful man in the community. But Slag gets on Rok's nerves, and so Rok continues his quest to find his own place. Eventually, he discovers an empty cave and invites his friends over for a cave-warming. When his friends leave, Rok is lonely and doesn't know what to do. Soc, the local wise man, suggests that Rok find female companionship, but, feeling that he doesn't understand women, Rok decides to return to his parents. On the way, he meets Pantha, a beautiful girl whom another man is trying to take for a mate. The man literally beats Rok into the ground but then leaves deciding that it is late and he has to return to his wife. Rok asks Pantha to move in with him. She agrees but first must retrieve some things from her cave. When she comes to Rok's cave, she brings her entire family – mother, father, sister, and brother. Rok leaves and returns to Mommy and Daddy. The next day, he sees a beautiful girl walk by his parent's cave and strolls off with her.

Corky/ Love Me, Love Queenie

In fall 1964, both writers Budd Grossman and Bob Schiller and Bob Weiskopf seemed to have worked on a comedy-fantasy project about a boy with extrasensory perception. The Grossman project was initially called *Seymour* and then *Corky*. The Schiller/Weiskopf proposal was labeled *Love Me, Love Queenie*. While the projects were for CBS, further details about them are unknown.

Frank Merriwell

Based on the Burt Standish books about the exploits of heroic Frank Merriwell, Leslie Stevens produced this late 1964 satirical comedy-adventure series starring Jeff Cooper.

The story line had Merriwell winning a sports car race against his antagonist played by Beau Bridges. The Bridges character hires two scoundrels to find out why Merriwell's car is so fast. They also take Merriwell's girl (Tisha Sterling) hostage and place her in the gondola of a runaway hot air balloon. Frank shimmies up the dangling tether line, punctures the balloon, and rescues the fair maiden.

ABC considered this vehicle for its 1965-66 prime-time schedule but ultimately passed on it.

This Desilu pilot was at least the second attempt to bring Standish's character to the small screen. In the 1950s, producers Tony London and Ira Uhr sought to produce a less humorous version of the Merriwell tales. The producers made arrangements with the University of Southern California to use two college grid squads to represent Harvard and Yale football teams for sequences in the proposed series.

The producers launched a nationwide search for a college-athlete type to play the lead. They indicated that "Merriwell will be as fearless, as intrepid and as valiantly undefeatable in TV as he was in his numerous novels."[58] London and Uhr found twenty-one-year-old Harry Craig to play Merriwell. Born in St. Louis, Missouri and raised in Dallas, Texas, Craig, who changed his first name to Larry, was attending USC at the time the producers signed him for the role.

EM + C2, Inc.

Developed by Norman Lessing, this 1964 effort attempted to combine science with comedy. The concept was submitted to CBS which decided not to turn it into a series.

The unproduced pilot centered on Cortelyou Carter, nicknamed C-Square who, along with a supercomputer named EMMA, and an assistant, Fairfax, headed a company that solved problems. His company's motto was "The Difficult we do at once; the Impossible takes a little longer." Cathy Norestrom was Carter's housekeeper.

In a pilot script by Lessing titled "Ten Arabs Named Herman," C-Square and Fairfax witness the assassination of a bodyguard for the King of Sauki Arabia. A State Department protocol officer, Lieutenant Detective Quill, King Ermani, his young son, his Prime Minster, and a Charge d'Affaires visit C-Square. To protect the King from assassination, EMMA provides a plan to have ten men all wearing the same costume impersonate his Highness on a flight to Washington D.C. The King's name in English is "Herman." C-Square elicits the King, his Prime Minster, Fairfax, Detective Quill, and himself to masquerade as the King along with five actors from central casting. On board the airplane, C-Square finds that there are eleven full-grown Arabs instead of ten. He surmises that one of the Arabs masquerading as the King plans to murder him. C-Square contacts EMMA to determine how to weed out the suspected assassin and who has hired him.

C-Square identifies the suspect who subsequently takes a passenger hostage at gun point. The King's ten-year-old son with a dagger, unnoticed by the assassin, strikes the assassin's hand that is holding the gun. C-Square then accuses the State Department protocol officer of being an enemy agent who hired the assassin.

EMMA had devised the plan for ferreting out the assassin by having everyone on the plane jot down their comments about the inflight movie. All the actors roundly criticized the leading man in the film, but the assassin didn't mention him. C-Square presumed the protocol officer was an impersonator when he ordered the stewardess to serve drinks to all the Arabs on board unaware that Arabs do not drink hard liquor.

Penelope's Boys

Proposed in October 1964, this comedy-Western, produced by Allen Miner and written by Norman Lessing, was presented to CBS for consideration. The network decided not to approve further development.

The pilot script dealt with a woman named Penelope who had been married to Big Joe, the murdered gang lord of Philadelphia. Penelope and Joe's "boys" moved West where she ran a saloon in Peaceful, population 675, and also became the town's sheriff with the boys as her deputies. Chowderhead, Little Iggy, Speed, and Curly were her deputies who kept Peaceful "peaceful."

The pilot, titled "A Kid Named Billy," dealt with Penelope receiving a letter that Big Joe's nephew Billy has taken the wrong path in life. Meanwhile, Little Iggy has obtained a reputation for his work with a gun, and so gunslingers are after him to prove that they are better at gunplay than he is. Billy the Kid is one of the gunfighters who comes to town to challenge Iggy. However, Penelope thinks that Billy is Big Joe's nephew and not the notorious gunslinger. She treats him like one of the family giving him a home-cooked meal and a bath. Billy the Kid sets up a showdown with Little Iggy. Come the day of the gunfight, both Little Iggy and Billy fire at the same time. Little Iggy rolls over on his back and looks very dead. As Billy leaves town, he gives Speed a letter for Penelope writing that he is not her nephew but is really Billy the Kid. Penelope says that she knew from the start that he was not her nephew and had substituted blanks in the Kid's gun in place of live ammunition. Little Iggy had just played dead.

Alfred of the Amazon

For CBS, this 1966 comedy pilot starred Wally Cox as Alfred, a man who has never done anything right. In this spoof of jungle films, Alfred is sent by his wealthy father to run a rubber plantation on the upper Amazon River. Arnie Rosen scripted the pilot.

The test show, titled "Two Shrunken Heads Are Better than One," had Alfred trying to rescue a pretty girl and her father from Yabanara headhunters. Costarring with Wally Cox were Paul Hartman as Dr. Schwimmer and Mako as Simba. The concept of the planned series had bumbling Alfred fighting injustice in his spare time.

Although *Alfred of the Amazon* never became a series, its star, Wally Cox, did have a featured role in the pilot for *Mission: Impossible* playing the character Terry Targo.

Chapter 17: Lucy's Unsold Drama Pilots

Despite success in selling *Star Trek*, *Mission: Impossible*, and *Mannix* to the networks, several other drama pilots made while Lucille Ball was in charge of Desilu were never picked up as a series.

Spellbound

In 1963, Desilu secured the title and music rights to the 1945 Hitchcock film, *Spellbound* about the new head of a mental hospital who is not whom he claims to be. Ralph Nelson attempted to come up with a concept for a series with this title. In 1964, Oscar Katz assigned Robert Blees to work out a premise for the series. Although NBC expressed some interest in the project, no concept let alone a pilot was ever developed.

The Greenhorns

For twelve months beginning in June 1963, Desilu tried to make a pilot for a Western series written by Charles Marquis Warren to be filmed in color. Dale Robertson was sought for one of the leads in the planned series.

Oscar Katz told *Variety* that this series would be the "most ambitious western ever groomed for tv."[59] He went on to note that the project is a kaleidoscopic oater which covers a twenty-five-year span in five years on television.

Set during the late 1860s, the project appears to have been about settlers on a wagon train journeying to the West. A treatment for the series starts out with a group of people participating in the first land rush in Kansas to claim territory held by the Indians. Among the families taking part in the land rush are the Cogswell's headed by Gib Cogswell and the Kilman's whose patriarch is a lawyer. Both families fail at staking a claim in the land grab, and so decide to join a wagon train with trail master, Smith Moran, to head farther West to find a place to settle.

NBC and ABC were approached to see if they were interested in the project, but ultimately, both networks rejected it.

Borderline

In summer 1964, Desilu considered a sixty-minute Western titled *Borderline* conceived by Robert Blees. The premise of the project is not known. It may have dealt with happenings on the border between the United States and Mexico.

Cleat Adams

Cleat Adams, a 1964 proposal to be produced by Martin Jurow with a pilot script to be done by George Eckstein, was a baseball adventure series dealing with a group of players. Beyond this brief description, nothing else could be found about the project except that, if a pilot had been made and had been picked up as a series, each episode would have been thirty minutes in length.

Escapade

This proposed thirty-minute adventure series to be produced by Allen Miner in 1964-65 involved four men on a sailing ship. This sea-going adventure was another project under Oscar Katz that never went anywhere.

Miner had previously written and directed several episodes of the long-running Western, *Wagon Train*.

The Long Hunt of April Savage

Before Oscar Katz left Desilu in 1966, three pilots were sold to the three networks at the time. For the 1966-67 season, *Mission: Impossible* was picked up by CBS, *Star Trek* was bought by NBC, and *The Long Hunt of April Savage* was purchased by ABC. ABC sought to schedule this thirty-minute Western starring Robert Lansing on Wednesdays at 9:00. However, the network ultimately decided against putting the series on its fall schedule and replaced it with *The Man Who Never Was*. Lansing starred in that series as well playing an American spy who takes on another man's identity.

The Long Hunt of April Savage had Robert Lansing playing the lead character who goes after a gang of eight murderers who had killed his family including his wife Elizabeth, his five-year-old daughter Sue Ann, and his seven-year-old son Jeff. The concept was that he would kill one of the murderers every eight episodes or so.

The eight killers were March Cole Savage, April's brother (the brothers' first names came from the month in which each was born); Sangaree; Alden Slade; Sir Ranald Beverly; Noah Delahanty; Daniel Henri; the Dancing Kid; and Clovis Beowulf. According to the Wanted Poster shown at the beginning of each proposed episode, Alden Slade had already been killed before the series would have premiered. The show would have lasted about four years with April Savage not only crossing America to track down the murderers of his family but also visiting other countries in his quest for vengeance.

In the prospectus for the planned series, Rolfe described the image of April Savage thusly in the opening of each episode:

> The Argentine poncho covers his body like a black shroud, flowing back in a trailing whiplash over the tail of the horse. A double barreled shotgun is cradled across the arm that grasps the reins, the other hand clamping the stock, finger curled around the twin triggers. Other details spring sharply to the eye – the bowie knife strapped to the outside of his right boot – the twin forty-fours hyphenating his thighs, their pistol grips thrust forward in readiness for a Border Draw.[60]

The pilot script, written by Sam Rolfe in September 1965 and titled "Home Is an Open Grave," had Savage returning to his ranch where his family is buried with one open grave for himself. He discovers a woman named Amelinda and her young daughter have taken over the bunk house on the property – the main house having burned down during the attack on his family. He is there to meet a man, Dandy Smith, who says he has information on the whereabouts of one of the murderers. Smith offers to tell April where April's brother March is who led the group of killers in return for Savage removing the name of Noah Delahanty from his list. In response to the offer, April says he will pay for information on the killers' location but not delete Delahanty from the list.

One of the three men who accompanied Smith to the ranch fires at Savage but misses. Savage fires back and doesn't miss. Dandy Smith and his two remaining friends have a box of dynamite hoping to blast April out of the bunk house along with Amelinda and her daughter. With Dandy throwing lighted sticks of dynamite at the bunk house, Savage begins firing at him and his friends. April and Amelinda shoot Dandy's two friends. April then gets the drop on Smith. The two begin fighting with April demanding that Smith divulge the whereabouts of March Savage and Noah Delahanty, but Smith is able to escape. One of Smith's friends, who was shot but is still alive, reveals that Dandy Smith is really Noah Delahanty.

Gene Roddenberry, who had written several scripts for Sam Rolfe's previous Western, *Have Gun, Will Travel*, produced this pilot for Desilu.

The Night Hunters

For the 1966-67 TV season, Desilu considered making another series created by Sam Rolfe about a retired New York City police commissioner who becomes a private investigator. The former commissioner, Max Chartreuse, now in his fifties, is the brains in his investigations and partners with John Dancer, a younger man who is the "brawn," specializing in the art of thievery. Max carries a gun but is a terrible shot; Dancer is a good marksman but has no permit for a gun.

While the pilot was apparently never produced, Rolfe drafted a script titled "The Hanged Men" that opens with a scene of a marriage ceremony between Michele Hoyt and Dennis Lowell when the body of a man hanging by a rope drops from the ceiling to the altar of the church. Chartreuse and his assistant, a pickpocket expert named David Lancer in the original draft script, take on the case to discover the killer because Max had received a letter from the deceased man, Calvin Lowell, Dennis Lowell's uncle, the day before Calvin was found hanged. Calvin Lowell, the wealthy head of Lowell Industries, had been drugged with chloral methylate before he was hanged. Chartreuse finds the same drug in a bottle of scotch about to be drunk by Dennis Lowell's father.

Unfortunately, the script from the Sam Rolfe collection at the American Heritage Center at the University of Wyoming ends before the murderer is revealed.

Chapter 18: Gene Roddenberry's Unsold and Rejected Desilu Pilots

The famous creator of *Star Trek*, Gene Roddenberry, had flown combat missions for the Army Air Force during World War II and, after the war, became a member of the Los Angeles Police Department. After quitting the LAPD to become a full-time writer, Roddenberry scripted several police, military, and Western TV series. While at Desilu, he developed several projects other than *Star Trek*.

High Noon

In July 1964, Roddenberry worked on a one-hour television version of the classic Western film starring Gary Cooper. *High Noon* was to pick up where the feature stopped.

The movie chronicled a morning in the life of Marshal Will Kane (Cooper) of Hadleyville, New Mexico, newly married to Amy Fowler (Grace Kelly). Kane is about to retire. However, he learns that Frank Miller (Ian MacDonald), an outlaw whom Kane had sent to prison, is being released and will arrive in town on the noon train. Miller and his gang are seeking revenge on the Marshal. No one in town wants to help Kane in facing the gang. Kane ends up subduing the outlaws with the help of his wife and then both leave Hadleyville.

The television version of the movie could have explored Kane and his wife's exploits in another town, or the effect on the people of Hadleyville in not assisting the Marshal with the Miller gang, or a combination of both.

By August 1964, ABC, which evidently had expressed some interest with the project, passed on it.

The Whirlwind

When Oscar Katz became production chief at Desilu, one of his first actions was to sign Gene Roddenberry to develop drama pilots for the company. One of the pilots was a thirty-minute Western to be titled *The Whirlwind*.

The project was to be a *Peyton Place*-style Western set sometime in the 1800s and dealing with the personal lives of the residents of a small town. Development began in October 1964. Supposedly, a script was written by Roddenberry, but a pilot was never made.

Code 100

Oscar Katz had Robert Blees and Gene Roddenberry work on developing this one-hour police drama in 1964, initially for ABC. At the beginning of development, the project was called *Assignment 100* and dealt with a Boston police officer with a limited time to live.

However, the script written by Blees for this drama focused on Detective Allen Paige, who reported directly to F.W. V. Harper, Superintendent of Police for a New England city. Paige has been given the assignment to end the gambling and bookmaking activities in the locale but has run up against numerous obstacles in pursuit of those running the operations. A police lieutenant, who was surveilling the drop-off of gambling revenue by a Joel Patten, ultimately dies of his wounds after a shoot-out with Patten whom the officer killed. Later, Paige and a Captain Keefer send in undercover officers to gain information on bookmaking activities at a liquor store, but someone tips off the operators leaving the police with no evidence.

Paige begins shadowing a man named Berg who, in court, claimed the gambling money that Patten was dropping off. Through a wiretap, the detective learns that the men behind the gambling operations are changing how they collect the winnings and deliver them to the head man. Paige and other detectives raid the office – the site of the drop-off, and confiscate $832,000 along with arresting Ivy, one of Patten's associates. A witness comes forward willing to testify against Ivy, but the witness is murdered before Ivy's trial gets underway. Paige's frustration over the investigation grows to the point of him deciding to take the $832,000 from the police property room hoping this will lure the mastermind of the gambling operation out into the open. Ivy, who is out on bail, and Berg track Paige's girlfriend, Dorian, to Paige's hiding place to take back the money. During a shoot-out between Paige and Ivy, the latter is killed. In the final scene, Paige returns the money to Harper.

When ABC passed on the project, NBC indicated interest but before the end of 1964 the project was tabled.

Blood, Of the A.E.F.

Another Gene Roddenberry project from 1964, this one-hour proposal concerned the American Expeditionary Force. The force had been formed by the U.S. Army on the Western Front during World War I under the command of Major General John J. Pershing. Just what the role would be of the lead character whose last name was "Blood" is not known.

Roddenberry had previously created the military series, *The Lieutenant*, for NBC. *Blood, Of the A.E.F.* was for CBS.

Police Story

Not to be confused with NBC's *Police Story* anthology from the 1970's, this 1965 pilot, written by Gene Roddenberry, was supposedly another iteration of the *Code 100* project. It focused on two detectives, James Page (Steve Ihnat) and Ed Questor (Gary Clarke) dealing with the case of a sniper who has shot one man and killed a woman. Prior to joining the police force, Page was a lawyer whose wife and child had been murdered.

In the pilot, the two detectives are also coping with a new chief (Malachi Throne) assigned to their department. Also, in the planned series was DeForest Kelly as Lab Chief Charlie Green.

Green finds that the bullet that killed the woman came from a pistol and not a shotgun being used by the sniper. The woman was shot dead before the sniper started his rampage. Page believes that she was killed by someone who knew her, and then the perpetrator started shooting others to draw attention to a "psycho" sniper. When the suspected sniper is sighted, all the police officers are called to the site. Page attempts to talk with the man about giving himself up. The suspect surrenders his gun as other officers try to shoot him. He turns out to be a part-time janitor but is not the sniper. The real killer is a man who lived with the woman who had been killed.

NBC considered picking up *Police Story* as a mid-season replacement during the 1967-68 season, but then dropped such plans.

Star Trek - "The Cage"

Jeffrey Hunter as Capt. Pike in a scene from "The Cage."

Development of *Star Trek* began in 1964 with creator Gene Roddenberry envisioning the prospective series as "built around characters who travel to worlds 'similar' to our own, and meet the action-adventure-drama which becomes our stories. Their transportation is the cruiser 'S.S. Yorktown', performing a well-defined and long-range Exploration-Science-Security mission which helps create our format."[61]

To reduce production costs for the planned series and to give viewers a frame of reference, Roddenberry developed the concept of "Parallel Worlds" meaning that the episodes would deal with life similar to that on earth.

Originally, the principal characters were defined by Roddenberry as follows:

Captain Robert M. April is about thirty-four years old whom Roddenberry described as a "space-age Captain Horatio Hornblower," whose primary weakness is a predilection to take action over administration;

The Executive Officer, referred to as "Number One," is a female who takes over from April as acting commander when he leaves the S.S. Yorktown. The character is extraordinarily efficient with a detailed knowledge of the systems, departments, and crew members aboard the vessel;

Jose Ortegas, a twenty-five-year-old born in South America, is the ship's navigator who fights an ongoing battle with the vessel's instruments and calculators;

Phillip "Bones" Boyce, the fifty-one-year old ship's doctor, is April's confidant who considers himself the only realist aboard the craft;

Mr. Spock, the ship's first lieutenant, is probably half Martian with a slightly reddish complexion and semi-pointed ears. He has a quiet temperament and is the nearest to Captain April's equal as a commander of men; and

Colt, the Captain's yeoman, a female, serves as April's secretary, reporter, and bookkeeper.

In his treatment for the series, Roddenberry also points out that while the S.S. Yorktown will rarely land on a planet, landings will be made via a small, transportable reconnaissance rocket.

The first *Star Trek* pilot went before cameras in November 1964 with Jeffrey Hunter as Captain Pike – not Captain April. Leonard Nimoy did appear as a more emotional Mr. Spock, the first lieutenant. John Hoyt played Dr. Phillip Boyce; Majel Barrett was Number 1; Peter Duryea had the role of Lieutenant Jose Tyler, the ship's navigator; and Laurel Goodwin appeared as Yeoman J. M. Colt, Pike's secretary.

By the time of the first pilot, the ship's name was changed from Yorktown to the Enterprise.

In the pilot, "The Cage," the Enterprise receives a distress signal from the S. S. Columbia which had crashed eighteen years earlier on Talos IV indicating that there are eleven survivors. Pike, Boyce, Spock, and three other crew transport to the planet where they encounter the human survivors watched over by a group of humanoids with bulbous craniums called the Talosians. The Talosians have brains three sizes larger than humans and communicate through mental telepathy. One survivor, the attractive Vina (Susan Oliver), who was born when the Columbia crashed, mesmerizes Pike. She takes him to the Talosians where he is captured.

The Talosians create illusions for their captives based on their captives' thoughts. They show Vina on another planet with Pike trying to protect her from fierce warriors. Pike realizes that it is an illusion but still engages the warrior in combat. Vina reveals that she is with the Captain to please him based on his dreams. When he questions her about the Talosians, she states that they can't make a person do anything that he or she would not ordinarily do but they can punish people for disobeying them. After the Talosians arrived on the planet, since they found little life on its surface, they went underground and developed their mental capacities. Vina indicates that she is to be "Eve" to Pike's "Adam." Pike theorizes that the Talosians want to create a group of human slaves to perform manual tasks on the planet's surface which they cannot do.

The Talosians invent various pleasurable fantasies for Pike with him picnicking with Vina and with Vina performing a sensual dance, but these illusions do not make Pike want to stay with Vina. The Captain blocks his thoughts with primitive urges like hatred so that the Talosians cannot read his mind. Pike is able to capture one of the Talosians who says he has to be released or the Enterprise will be destroyed. Meanwhile, Number 1 and other crew members transport themselves to inside the Talosians' headquarters. However, only the two women – Number 1 and Yeoman Colt actually appear to Pike. After the Captain calls the Talosians bluff about destroying the Enterprise, he escapes with Number 1 and Yeoman Colt to the planet's surface where Number 1 says that she will destroy herself and the other humans unless they are permitted to go back to their ship. The Talosians decide that, because humans prefer death over captivity, the Captain, Number 1, and the Yeoman can return to the Enterprise. With the illusions terminated, Vina is shown to transform into a disfigured old lady as Pike goes back to his ship. The Talosians had attempted to make her whole when they discovered her in the wreckage of the Columbia but they had no guide as to what humans looked like.

NBC rejected the pilot as being too cerebral and lacking action. Herb Solow pointed out other reasons the network opposed "The Cage." "NBC was very concerned with the 'eroticism' of the pilot and what it foreshadowed for the ensuing series. Their knowledge of Roddenberry's attitude toward, and relationship with, the fairer sex didn't help. NBC Sales was equally concerned about the Mister Spock character, him being seen as demonic by Bible Belt affiliate-station owners and important advertisers."[62]

However, the network did give the go ahead to Desilu to produce another pilot titled "Where No Man Has Gone Before" which became the first episode of *Star Trek* to be aired with an entirely new cast except for Leonard Nimoy. William Shatner starred as Capt. James T. Kirk when Jeffrey Hunter decided not to renew his contract. The characters of Number 1, Dr. Boyce, Yeoman Colt, and Lieut. Jose Tyler were eliminated and the characters of Dr. Leonard McCoy, Sulu, Uhura, and Engineer Montgomery Scott were added.

Even though the initial three-year run for the original *Star Trek* was not a ratings winner, the subsequent TV spin-offs, feature films, and merchandising made the series one of the most profitable in the history of television.

Assignment: Earth

Before Desilu was sold to Gulf and Western Industries in February 1967, Gene Roddenberry began developing a thirty-minute time travel series called *Assignment: Earth*. The first draft script, dated November 14, 1966, focused on Gary (originally "Anthony") Seven, born in the year 2319 who travels back in time to Earth 1967 to fight the evil Omegans. The evildoers have sent a group of agents to Earth to lay the groundwork for taking over the planet.[63]

Seven has rented an office to establish a private detective agency from which he will work to defeat the Omegans and is looking for a secretary. Roberta "Bobbi" Hornblower applies for the position and is hired by Seven. Harth and Isis, two of the Omegan agents, observe the activities in the "7-Agency" through their crystal. They attempt, unsuccessfully, to kill both Seven and Roberta.

In the process of developing this project, the concept appears to have been expanded to have the Seven character traveling to Earth to protect the planet from destroying itself instead of only fighting the evil Omegans.

Star Trek was pitched to the networks as *"Wagon Train* to the stars." *Wagon Train* had been a successful Western on NBC and then ABC each week focusing on a different story about settlers traveling to the West. For *Assignment: Earth*, Roddenberry described the planned series as *"Have Gun-Will Travel, 1968."* He had written several scripts for Richard Boone's Western about a gunfighter for hire named Paladin. In his letter to NBC about the show, Roddenberry wrote, "The prime dramatic ingredients of both shows are almost identical – both shows feature a slightly larger-than-life main character, who sallies forth weekly from a familiar 'home base' to do battle with extraordinary evil in an action-adventure format."[64]

After the sale of Desilu, "Assignment: Earth" was made as a potential spin-off from *Star Trek* with Robert Lansing and Teri Garr in the lead roles. On the episode airing March 29, 1968, the Enterprise returns to Earth on a research project to learn more about the planet's shaky survival in the year 1968. The crew encounters Gary Seven and questions his explanation of his mission and the urgency of getting to work immediately since a nuclear bomb is being readied for launch.

NBC failed to turn the pilot into a series.

Yankee Gunfighter

Details are scare about this Gene Roddenberry project for Desilu. *Yankee Gunfighter* appears to have been a thirty-minute, never-produced-Western pilot for CBS. It may very well have been another iteration of *Have Gun-Will Travel* about a gunfighter who contracted with people to go up against their enemies.

Chapter 19: Precursors to Mission: Impossible

Premiering on September 17, 1966 on CBS, *Mission: Impossible* focused on a group of specialized government agents carrying out complex missions to disrupt the plans of foreign countries who sought to create problems for the United States or its allies. Known as the Impossible Mission Force, the team consisted of Steven Hill as Daniel Briggs, the leader, Greg Morris as Barney Collier, the electronics expert, Barbara Bain as Cinnamon Carter, the femme fatale, Martin Landau as Rollin Hand, a master of disguise, and Peter Lupus as Willie Armitage, the muscular strong man. Over its run on television, various members of the IMF team came and went.

The original treatment for *Mission: Impossible*, titled "Briggs' Squad: A Beginning", written by Bruce Geller in 1965, included the following characters as part of Lt. Col. David (not Daniel) Briggs' (ret.) special squad:

Albert Key, a wheeler-dealer, is adept at knowing where to find needed material, what it costs, and how to find the money to buy it;

Jack Smith, a ladies-man, has never worked a day in his life and specializes in getting what he wants from women;

Barney Collier, with graduate degrees in bio-electro chemical engineering, permutative mathematics, and micro-physics, is an expert in ballistics, demolition, and submarine vessels as well as being a compulsive gambler;

Willy Armitage, nicknamed "Arm," ugly, ill-educated, inept, is the strongest man in the world;

Little Terry Targo, soft-spoken and mild-mannered, is a master at all forms of hand-to-hand combat and works as a professional hitman; and

Martin Land, known as the "Great Martin," is a master of disguise, a quick change artist, and fluent in fifteen languages.

Briggs himself is described as an expert in human beings with a doctorate in analytical psychology and highly paid as a behavioral analyst. He once led the group of characters described above when they were all part of the same Special Forces group.

When the pilot for *Mission: Impossible* was made, in addition to the Briggs character, only the characters of Barney Collier, Willy Armitage, Terry Targo, and Martin Land, now named Rollin Hand, appeared along with the addition of Cinnamon Carter. The Terry Targo character, played by Wally Cox, was featured only in the pilot.

There were two pilots produced by Desilu before *Mission: Impossible* that had striking similarities to the concept for that series.

The Man Nobody Knows

Created by Hendrik Vollaerts, this project was intended for syndication. It dealt with a super-investigator who operates out of Washington D.C. and works in a quasi-official capacity for an unidentified bureau. The proposed series, initially called *Man with 1000 Faces,* starred Steve Peck as the investigator who would play a different person each week. Peck would open and close each installment.

In the pilot, Ralph Logan (Peck) works for the Office of Security in Washington D.C. Logan is given the mission to arrest members of a group producing and distributing fake American passports. He disguises himself as Carl Hartog, the leader of the group forging the documents. The real Hartog is arrested by agents accompanying Logan. Logan then has to catch and arrest Hartog's accomplices. Disguised as Hartog, Logan is able to find the plates used in producing the passports and arrest the other members of the gang.

In his autobiography, Desi Arnaz opined that this planned series was "the basis of *Mission: Impossible.*"[65] Like Roland Hand (Martin Landau) in *Mission: Impossible,* Peck's character would don make-up at the beginning of the episode to appear as someone else and then have another actor actually play that character. This adventure series began development in 1957 with a pilot finally made in 1959.

Trio

This Desilu project dealt with the adventures of three ex-Army friends who live in different sections of the United States but meet in various locales to help individuals and governments in times of trouble. The team included an engineer, a lawyer, and a doctor.

In the 1958 pilot script, written by Ed Adamson, the three troubleshooters go to a Latin American country to track down a group of hijackers who have stolen the government's treasury.

After a year passed, Martin Leeds revived the project in January 1959, but a few months later, it was dropped again.

However, the real precursor to *Mission: Impossible* was a short-lived series made by Filmways in the late 1950s titled *21 Beacon Street*. *21 Beacon Street* focused on a team of operatives who devised elaborate schemes for catching criminals. Dennis Chase (Dennis Morgan) was the head of the team, Lola (Joanna Barnes) was the female operative; and Randy Burke (Brian Kelly) was simply named "Brian," a law school graduate. James Maloney as Jim, dialectician and scientific expert, rounded out the cast.

Episodes of *21 Beacon Street* dealt with schemes such as using closed circuit television to help find a crime syndicate's payroll list; devising a hoax to swindle a con man out of money that he had taken from a widow; and having Chase pose as a member of an international narcotics ring to track down the killer of an undercover agent.

Leonard Heideman created *21 Beacon Street*. Apparently work and family stress caused Heideman to have a psychotic episode and on February 23, 1963, he stabbed his wife Dolores to death. Declared unfit to stand trial, he was committed for an indefinite period to the Atascadero State Hospital in California. Heideman spent fourteen months there. After he pled not guilty by reason of insanity to his wife's murder, and the hospital staff testified that he had fully recovered from his psychosis, he became a free man and changed his name to Laurence Heath. Heath wrote an account of his crime, trial, and treatment titled *By Reason of Insanity* published in 1966. He subsequently began scripting episodes of *Mission: Impossible*.

Bruce Geller, the creator of *Mission: Impossible*, was sued by Filmways in 1968. Filmways claimed that *Mission: Impossible* resembled *21 Beacon Street* in its emphasis on gadgetry and a team of experts. Geller said he had never seen *21 Beacon Street*, but he paid Filmways off anyway to settle the suit.

Chapter 20: Desi Arnaz Productions

In the late 1960s, Desi Arnaz rented space at the Desilu Culver studios from his former wife to begin producing his own projects again. In 1966, Arnaz envisioned making a movie titled *Without Consent* starring Spencer Tracy as well as a television special starring Cantinflas. Neither project came to fruition.

The Cantinflas project would have been a sixty-minute special with the comic touring his home country of Mexico. Speculation was that if the Cantinflas special had been successful, other specials with stars from countries like Brazil and Argentina would have been made by Desi.

The Mothers-in-Law was the only pilot Desi Arnaz produced under his own company that became a series. The show starred Eve Arden as Eve Hubbard with Herb Rudley playing her lawyer-husband. Kaye Ballard appeared as Kaye Buell, whose husband, initially played by Roger C. Carmel and then Richard Deacon, was a TV script writer. Originally, Ann Sothern was considered as a co-star for *The Mothers-in-Law*, but her and Eve Arden's acting styles were similar, and so Kaye Ballard came on board as an Italian Lucy-type character as a counterpoint to Arden's Anglo-Saxon Lucy.

After being rejected by CBS, the series was sold to NBC and ran for two seasons. The show's original pilot never aired. Like the first episode of the series that was broadcast, the pilot told the story of how Eve's daughter, Susie, and Kaye's son, Jerry, became engaged and then married before their mothers had a chance to give them the wedding the mothers thought appropriate. Jerry Fogel played Kaye's son; Kay Cole appeared as Eve's daughter. But the role of Susie was recast with Deborah Walley, and so the pilot with Kay Cole never aired.

Reflecting on the series, Desi Arnaz wrote:

I never forgot Bob Carroll Jr. and Madelyn Davis, who wrote the "I Love Lucy" shows 180 times without repeating themselves, and I never forgot Eve Arden, who used to film "Our Miss Brooks" right next door to where we did "I Love Lucy."

Having never forgotten these three people, I came back to Hollywood on the old fire horse, locked them all in an office with two lawyers and six contract negotiators and on September 10 we went on the air with the first episode...

Arnaz further commented, "There is nothing 'new' or 'different' about 'The Mothers-in-Law,' any more than there is anything new or different about the circus or about the way people laugh. People laugh at something funny, and 'The Mothers-in-Law' is funny. That's all it is. It doesn't pretend to be anything else. And as far as I'm concerned we need laughter today more than we have ever needed it before."[66]

Many of the plots reminded one of *I Love Lucy*. For instance, in "I Haven't Got a Secret," Rodger sells a soap opera he has created to a television network. He forbids Kaye to inform anyone about the sale until it is finalized thinking that blabbing about it will jinx the project. Naturally, Kaye can't wait to make Eve aware of the news, but, taking into account Rodger's admonition, Kaye, in a Lucy-like way, pantomimes the secret for Eve. Eve, in turn, does the same pantomime with Herb. Kaye then starts thinking about how she will spend all the money she anticipates Rodger will get for the series and goes on a buying spree. Of course, when Rodger returns home, he tells everyone that the deal fell through.

The Mothers-in-Law also continued the show business theme of many of Desi's sitcoms and comedy pilots even though the characters, except for Rodger, were not really involved in the entertainment field. In "Career Girls," Eve and Kaye decide to stop interfering in the lives of their married children and look for work. Kaye had been a Big Band singer with some little-known bands, while Eve had performed on the stage in college. They work up a country-western act and sing at a local cabaret. In the end, the two quit show business when the cabaret closes.

The entire cast got into the act in an episode, "My Son, the Actor." Jerry decides to become an actor when an aptitude exam he took indicates he has an interest in the arts. He tries out for the lead in a college musical performing a play his father wrote, *Marvin against the Mob* – a take-off on the 1920s gangster era. Kaye, Rodger, Eve, Herb, and Susie all perform in the audition along with Jerry who seems to have a smaller part than everyone else. Nevertheless, Jerry wins the lead role in the college musical but decides not to be an actor. He becomes a political science major.

With his own company, Desi also had several project ideas that never became a series.

The Carol Channing Show

Written by Madelyn Davis and Bob Carroll, Jr. and directed by Arnaz, *The Carol Channing Show* was another attempt to base a "Lucy-like" sitcom on a scatterbrained character who hopes to make it big in show business. Carol Honeycutt (Carol Channing) traveled to New York City from a small town hoping to become a star. After she has run out of money, she becomes homeless and hungry. In the park, she attempts to take a candy bar from a young boy (Jimmy Garrett) and eat hot dogs from a romantic couple while they are kissing. Florence (Jane Dulo), one of Carol's friends, sees her in the park and invites Carol to stay with her and her husband, Leon Thatcher (Richard Deacon), a New York mounted police officer who works nights.

Carol moves into Florence's apartment unbeknownst to Leon. Thinking the place is being burgled, Leon investigates and ends up shooting his toe. The Richard Deacon character, being the Fred Mertz/ Mr. Mooney type in the pilot, wants Carol to move out as soon as possible, and so he gets her a job as a waitress in an Italian restaurant where she creates all sort of problems trying to slice a ham with an electric knife. She is fired and returns to the Thatcher's while Leon is cleaning his gun causing him to shoot himself again in another toe.

Carol finally finds a job working as a taxi dancer at Dance Land where men pay her for each dance. She attempts to look sexy to entice men to dance with her. Initially, Carol has no luck, but then a sailor asks her to dance. Before finishing the number, the sailor leaves for a moment, and a succession of men dance with Carol performing a variety of different routines including a tango with an un-billed thirteen-year-old Desi Arnaz Jr. When the sailor comes back to finish his dance with Carol, she begs off saying she is too tired. Another man agrees with her, but the sailor persists causing a fight to break out wrecking the place with Leon, in his role as police officer, breaking up the altercation.

Ms. Channing was under contract with General Foods which persuaded CBS to share half the cost of the $500,000 to make this pilot. Reportedly, the network did not like the result but since General Foods was such a big advertiser, CBS agreed to schedule the show at 9:30 Tuesdays. The network warned the sponsor that the show "would be another *Jean Arthur Show* bust" which would last only six weeks. General Foods then offered the series to other networks. NBC said that "it wasn't that bad. . . worse things have been on. But they were trying to be like Lucille Ball and couldn't quite bring it off.[67]"The series was also presented to ABC but didn't get passed preliminary discussions.

Gussie, My Girl (second attempt)

This project, originally considered when Arnaz was head of Desilu, was resurrected as a possible series by Desi's new production company. Working again with writers Madelyn Davis and Bob Carroll, Jr, the concept involved another show business-themed comedy about a former vaudevillian, Oscar Gibson, and his single daughter Gussie who, encouraged by her father, sought to pursue a career in the entertainment field as a singer. Gussie's boyfriend, Hank Miller, a high school football coach, wants to marry her but only if she abandons her career.

In this proposal, Oscar Gibson was similar to the Fred Mertz character in *I Love Lucy* being formerly in show business and now owning a duplex in which he and his daughter lived and earned money from renting the rest of the duplex. Gussie was in the Lucy Ricardo mold engaging in broad comedy with a boyfriend similar to Ricky Ricardo who wanted a full-time wife with no show business career.

The pilot script had Oscar objecting to Gussie performing on a live variety show since she would be the first performer and he wanted her to go on next to last. The producer cancels her performance, but dad is able to get Gussie back in the show. Nevertheless, she decides to give up show business altogether and marry Hank. After Hank leaves, Gussie reconsiders appearing with her father and decides to perform one last time since Hank will be out of town at a football game. Hank returns to see Gussie and give her an engagement ring while she is in a cat costume. She beats a hasty retreat to her bedroom so he doesn't see her, but Hank discovers that she is wearing the costume and that she still wants to perform. He walks out on her.

On the night of the performance, Oscar and Gussie do a soft shoe number and sing "Honeysuckle Rose," and then do a rock and roll version of the song. Hank sees their act and apologizes for walking out on Gussie. Ed Sullivan was in the audience and wants Oscar and Gussie to perform on his TV show. Hank is resigned to the fact that Gussie's show business career will continue.

Davis and Carroll Jr. outlined several story possibilities for additional episodes of *Gussie and Me* including:

Gussie needs special material for her act and wants to hire a writer. Oscar says that he will write the material for her to save her money. What he comes up with is so corny she doesn't want to tell him and so secretly meets with a special materials writer to revise what her father had done. Dad finds out about the meetings and informs Hank that Gussie is seeing another man. Hank and Oscar follow them to see what is going on.

Oscar invites some old friends from vaudeville to stay with him and Gussie until they get back on their feet. The three men, who are acrobats, can't find any work. Gussie ends up cooking and doing their laundry. Meanwhile, the Gibson's living room has a huge trampoline in the middle. Gussie discovers that all of the men can sing very well. With her father filling in as a baritone, she has them booked at a neighborhood bar as a barbershop quartet.

Gussie goes to Hank's school to tell him something important. She looks for him in the boys' locker room. While there, the football team comes off the field to shower. Gussie hides in a locker and finally makes her escape dressed in an outsized sweat suit and a helmet.

Not known is if Janis Paige would play Gussie as she did in the prior incarnation of this proposed series. Jimmy Durante as well as Ken Murray were considered for the role of Gussie's father.

If the pilot had become a series and lasted for more than one season, Davis and Carroll Jr. contemplated Gussie and Hank marrying with Gussie's father living with them.

Ham and Davey

Another show that Desi considered making concerned the adventures of two stockcar drivers – David Bruce, a cautious, suspicious sort and

Hamilton Robson, an honest, independent young man. Their friendship began while preparing to race in the Southern 500. Ham is in the pit next to Davey and points out to him that one of his cars will not qualify for the race because it has an illegal front axle. Ham offers to sell an axle to Davey in exchange for old tires from Davey's other car.

As far as can be determined, the project was never cast and a pilot never made.

Land's End

Created and produced by Desi Arnaz and Mort Briskin, this thirty-minute adventure series pilot concerned Mark Daniels (Rory Calhoun), owner of the Baja-based Land's End Hotel that was managed by Linda Ware (Leigh Chapman).

In the pilot, Mark rescues a man named Eric (Martin Milner) after his boat explodes. Eric had three passengers on board – a young girl and her parents. Mark goes out searching for survivors and finds Jeannie, the young teen, clinging to some debris. She is taken care of at the hotel and put in an oxygen tent. Mark Daniels is suspicious of the cause of the boat explosion. Later, a friend of Mark's finds a valuable necklace on the beach where Eric was picked up. Mark and police captain Bravo (Gilbert Roland) find other jewelry in the same place. Subsequently, Eric breaks into Jeannie's room and turns off her oxygen. Mark and Bravo find her just in time, and Mark goes after Eric. Eric attempts to flee but falls off a cliff to his death. Evidently, Eric planned the explosion to steal the family's jewels.

Desi Arnaz wrote the music and lyrics for the show's theme song, "I Love You." The pilot was filmed in Baja, California. Arnaz considered La Paz, the capital of Baja, to be his home away from home. NBC aired the show in place of *The Mothers-in-Law* on April 21, 1968.

Chairman of the Board

In the early 1970's, Desi Arnaz was invited by Lew Wasserman, the head of MCA/Universal, to move his production company to Universal and develop potential series. One outcome of this new arrangement was a project titled *Chairman of the Board*, initially slated as a comeback vehicle for Arnaz.

While a script was written, no pilot appears to have been filmed. The story takes place in New York City where Desi's character – Desi Ranaldo, is proprietor of a bar and grill. In the opening, Desi is waiting on two regular customers - Marvin Holman, an attorney and a Mr. Randolph, a business owner. Randolph likes Desi's common sense and math skills.

Marvin and Randolph usually have drinks together every afternoon, but a week goes by and Randolph has been absent. A Mr. Mitchell visits the bar to inform Desi that Randolph has passed away from a heart attack. He invites Desi to come to his office the next day. When Desi arrives, he learns he is there for a reading of Randolph's will. Desi has been bequeathed 51% of the outstanding stock in Randolph Electric Industries, a manufacturer of electric appliances.

Oscar "Oz" Cushing, who is the President of the company, tries to convince Desi to sell his stock which would bring him over $100 million. Desi discusses the deal with Marvin Holman who convinces him to keep the stock and become the company's chairman of the board. The next day, Desi visits the executive offices of Randolph Electric and meets his secretary, Nancy Barons. Oz, speaking to the company's vice presidents, says he plans to run the firm as if Desi is not there. However, Desi sends memorandums to all the vice presidents instructing them to inform him in advance of any meetings. Oz suggests letting the company lose business and then blame Desi so that he can be removed from the board.

The next day, Desi arrives at the company and sees men picketing with signs stating that "Randolph Electric is Unfair to Organized Labor." Workers go on strike demanding a raise and more benefits. After the strike goes on for a month, Desi arranges a meeting with the union boss at his bar. They work out a deal to end the strike benefiting both the company and the workers. Oz and the vice presidents can't believe that Desi made such a good deal with labor.

At some point in the development of this project, Desi Arnaz decided not to play the lead character. The script was apparently rewritten to feature a female chairwoman of the board to be played by Elke Sommers.

Dr. Domingo

While at Universal, Desi Arnaz appeared in a one-hour drama that was to be a spin-off from Raymond Burr's *Ironside* to be called *Dr. Domingo*.

According to Arnaz, he got the idea for playing this character from an old paperback mystery which someone had left in his Baja California house.

Desi Arnaz with Patricia Smith in a scene from Dr. Domingo.

Juan Domingo is a Cuban refugee doctor with a knack for detective work. He is a physician in a small Northern California town where he acts as the local coroner. "He's a cross between Marcus Welby and Columbo," said Arnaz at the time.[68]

The *Ironside* episode, "Riddle at 24,000," aired March 21, 1974. It involved Dr. Domingo refusing to sign a death certificate when the pilot of a private plane appears to have died of a heart attack aloft. Domingo believes the man was murdered.

This was Desi Arnaz's final appearance in a dramatic role on a television series.

Chapter 21: Lucille Ball Productions

After the sale of Desilu to Gulf and Western Industries in 1967, Lucille Ball formed her own production company in February 1968 to make her third situation comedy.

Premiering in September 1968, *Here's Lucy* starred Ms. Ball playing Lucy Carter, a widow with two children – Kim and Craig portrayed by her real-life kids, Lucie Arnaz and Desi Arnaz Jr. Gale Gordon appeared as her brother-in-law Harry who owned the Unique Employment Agency where Lucy worked and became involved in typical "Lucy" situations.

In addition to a few pilots described later, Lucille Ball Productions sought to produce a special with Jackie Gleason based on the real-life characters of Diamond Jim Brady and Lillian Russell.

"Diamond Jim and Lillian Russell"

One project that Ms. Ball had wanted to do for a number of years concerned the relationship between Diamond Jim Brady to be played by Jackie Gleason and Lillian Russell with Lucy herself in that role. Newspapers reported in 1968 that Gleason and Ball would film Diamond Jim Brady in Florida beginning January 1969. Subsequently, papers indicated that the project would start production in March 1970. In October 1970, columnist Marilyn Beck wrote:

> Look for Jackie Gleason and Lucille Ball to reactivate those plans to star in the big-screen story of big Diamond Jim Brady and his Lillian Russell.
>
> They were talking about rolling with the film last year, but could never resolve whether Lucy would come to the Great One's Miami Beach mountain, or whether Gleason would

bow to Lucy and agree to shoot in Hollywood, where she TV-toils.

Now that problem's been solved. Jackie, courtesy of CBS canceling his show, no longer is tied to Florida.[69]

This ad for Lucille Ball Productions contains a blurb for the never-produced TV special, "Diamond Jim and Lillian Russell."

A script was done by *The Lucy Show* and *Here's Lucy* writer, Bob O'Brien for what was to originally be a feature film but then evolved into a TV spectacular. The project was never made. The concept was a musical comedy with Gleason and Ball performing songs from the era incorporated into the story line, with the emphasis more on "music" than on "comedy."

In O'Brien's first draft script, the setting is New York City in the 1890's. Lillian Russell is performing at one of the city's most fashionable theaters. She is singing "I'm in Love with a Man Named, Manhattan." Lillian is really in love with the orchestra leader, Felix Graham. During her song,

Diamond Jim Brady enters the theater with his entourage – Dr. Bodine, his doctor, and his wife; Harry Hutchins, a railroad magnate, and his wife; Charles A. Moore, a railroad supply executive; Jules Weiss, Jim's tailor and lifelong friend; and Kathy Cartwright, Jim's fiancée. Jim earned his fortune by selling railroad supplies for Harry Hutchins. Lillian stops singing as Jim opens a large box of chocolates and offers them to his friends. She is fascinated by his presence, and he offers her a chocolate to apologize for stopping the show.

Referring to the diamonds that he is wearing, Lillian says that when Brady stands up, he looks like a "lighthouse." To which he replies that he is built more like a "roundhouse." After the show, Jim visits Lil in her dressing room to remark how much he liked her performance. He invites her to an after-theater dinner party.

Jim and Kathy along with Lillian and Felix make a grand entrance at the party. Jim mentions that his horse "Gold Heels" is running in a race the next day. Lil loves horses. For himself, Jim, a hearty eater, orders a dozen cold lobsters, poached salmon, a leg of lamb, a saddle of venison, baked potatoes, and a couple dozen ears of corn. Jim and Lillian dance the night away with Kathy and Felix looking on. Felix sees Kathy to her home leaving Jim and Lil to dance.

The next day, Jim apologizes to Kathy for ignoring her the preceding night. Kathy says she is feeling under the weather and so doesn't want to accompany him to the horse race. Jim invites Lillian and Felix, but the latter doesn't want to go because he is seeking to finish a new musical he is writing.

Cynthia Leonard, Lillian's mother, stops by her place. Lillian's real name is Helen Leonard. Cynthia is one of the nation's leading feminists championing the suffragette movement, but she disdains her daughter's career in show business. While Lillian is dressing, Brady comes by and meets Cynthia. He tells Lillian's mother that she should be proud of her daughter's career.

Before the race, Lillian and Jim stop by the theater where Felix is working on his musical. They are surprised to see Kathy with Felix and conclude that the two have fallen in love. Jim and Lillian quietly exit as both admit that each wants what is right for their fiancées.

At the race, Lil runs into Jeffrey Daniels, her beau before she met Felix. She mentions that her planned wedding with Felix is off. Jim's horse is up against Satan's Brother in a match race. Although Satan's Brother is the favorite, Gold Heels comes from behind to win.

During the celebration after the race, an inebriated Daniels begins singing "He's a Jolly Good Fellow" embarrassing Lillian. Producer Flo Ziegfeld is at the party and asks to meet Felix whom Jim has told him about. As Lil is about to apologize for Felix's absence, he appears along with Kathy. After he plays the title song from the musical he wrote, Ziegfeld agrees to back the production.

A few days later on election night 1896, Cynthia Leonard is attempting to interest people in supporting the suffrage movement, but she elicits little excitement. Jim and Lil come by in a large wagon with marchers following and park close to the platform where Mrs. Leonard was speaking. Brady expresses support for the cause and introduces Lil to sing. People start signing the suffragette petition.

Next, a montage of brief pictorials, covering over a year, show Jim and Lillian enjoying life – riding in a hot air balloon, driving a horseless carriage, and sleighing in the snow. After the passage of time, Jim wants to ask Lillian to marry him. He broaches the subject with her in an off-hand manner, but she doesn't catch on. He thinks she still loves Jeff Daniels. Figuring that Lillian doesn't love him, he plans to sail to Europe.

Jim visits her before the ship departs. During the visit, a waiter that Lillian knows informs her that Daniels has been doing nothing but drinking his life away. Lillian goes to see him. What she finds is Jeffrey looking resplendent, prosperous, and completely sober. He had made up the story related by the waiter in order to ask Lil to dinner and celebrate his headlining a new production. He requests Lil's hand in marriage and mentions that it was Jim who got him on the "straight and narrow." Upon learning of Jim's involvement in helping Jeff, Lil turns down the marriage proposal.

As Jim is ready to depart on his trip to Europe, Lillian visits him and says that she is planning to marry. She notes that Jim always said that she would find a guy who was "okay." Lil then presents him with a gift of cuff links with the letter "O" on one and the letter "K" on the other. The couple becomes engaged. Jim buys Lil an expensive ring singing "There's that Has 'Em, Wears 'Em" with the entire cast joining in at the end.

In real life, Jim Brady never married. Lillian Russell was married four different times.

Although Gleason and Ball never made this project, they did appear together in 1975 in a Lucille Ball special, "Three for Two" – three playlets about marriage. In the first segment, "Herb and Sally," a mature couple is vacationing in Rome. Sally is looking forward to a romantic evening with her husband who just wants to sleep. They begin to argue about their years together, but make up in the end. In "Fred and Rita," Gleason and Ball are having an extramarital affair. They rendezvous in a darkened restaurant trying to plan an entire weekend together but their schedules don't permit. The last playlet, "Mike and Pauline," is set during New Year's Eve with the married couple arguing with their grown teenagers about their tradition of spending the night together. Their teens each want to go out. Pauline talks with her daughter who reveals she is engaged. The son speaks with his father about wanting to quit college and become a stand-up comic. In the end, the parents support their kids who go out leaving Mike and Pauline to celebrate New Year's Eve by themselves.

Viewers and critics alike were not enthused with this comedy-drama special in which both Lucy and Jackie departed from their usual TV personas.

The Lucie Arnaz Show (aka Kim)

In the twentieth episode of season four of *Here's Lucy* titled "Kim Moves Out," Kim dates Peter Sullivan (Tim Matheson). Lucy worries when Kim is late in coming home from her date. After all, Peter is a writer with a beard which apparently means that he can't be trusted. When Kim comes home, Lucy is asleep on the couch. Kim covers her with a blanket and goes out early the next day to have breakfast with Peter. Although Lucy thinks that Kim stayed out all night, Kim points out that Lucy had a blanket over her when she woke up proving her daughter came home. Kim remarks that her mother treats her like a little girl and decides to move out.

Lucy suggests that Kim take an apartment over the neighbor's garage. Kim moves, but her mother still comes by every day to help. Uncle Harry suggests that Kim change the locks so Lucy can't visit every day. With the locks changed, Lucy decides to use her ladder to enter the apartment through the window. She hides in the fireplace when Kim and Peter come home. Uncle Harry calls asking for Lucy and says she is probably hiding somewhere in the apartment. Kim thinks her mother is in the fireplace, and, to make a point, she sings several songs to keep her mother there. Finally, she says she is going to build a fire which prompts Lucy to reveal herself.

This episode was a precursor to the final episode of season four titled "Kim Finally Cuts You-Know-Who's Apron Strings" which was the pilot for Lucie Arnaz's own series. In that episode, written by Madelyn Davis and Bob Carroll Jr. and directed by Coby Ruskin, Kim has moved to an apartment at Marina Del Ray managed by Lucy's brother Herb Hinkley (Alan Oppenheimer), an amateur songwriter. She is working for a public relations firm and has met a British race car driver, Ronnie Cumberland (Lloyd Batista) at an auto show. Lucy has given Kim a book on self-defense, and she practices some tactics with her friend and neighbor Sue Ann Ditbenner (Susan Tolsky) - a tour guide at the Museum of History.

Kim goes out on a date with Ronnie who takes her to a movie about the Indianapolis 500. They come back to her apartment but are then interrupted by Herb and Sue. When Ronnie leaves early, Kim is mad at Sue and her uncle for barging in. The next night, after Kim and Ronnie have a candlelight dinner, he comes on to her too strongly. She has to use her self-defense tactics to get rid of him.

This episode of *Here's Lucy*, which aired February 21, 1972, ranked twenty-sixth for the week. While the pilot never became a series, Lucie Arnaz did subsequently star in her own self-titled comedy in April, 1985. She played a young single psychologist Jane Lucas, who writes a newspaper advice column and co-hosts a radio call-in show in addition to having her own private practice. The series was adapted from a British sitcom called *Agony* but lasted for only six episodes on CBS.

The Music Mart

As Lucille Ball related to Associated Press television writer Peter J. Boyer in early 1980, "Fred Silverman (NBC's President) asked me if I would come to NBC. I told him no, that I probably wouldn't leave CBS." The actress went on to say, "He asked me if I'd like to search for a half-hour sitcom for NBC. I thought, Gee, I wouldn't mind doing that, you know, producing. He asked me if I had any ideas"[70]

Out of that conversation, grew a ninety-minute special called "Lucy Moves to NBC" with Lucy playing herself as a producer developing a situation comedy starring Donald O'Connor, as Wally Coogan, a former Big

Band singer running a music store with his wife Carol (Gloria DeHaven) and son Scotty (Scotty Plummer).

The comedy attempt was really a throwback to the early 1950's with the trite story line of a father who likes music from the 1940's and a son who prefers contemporary sounds. Wally Coogan detests electric instruments and amplifiers. To make the son's music as bad as possible, the writers had Scotty's band play a cacophony of sounds to show viewers that modern music was simply noise. Further illustrating the cringeworthy nature of the pilot, the music store's black assistant was named "Ivory."

The story concerned Wally and Carol discussing a birthday gift for their son. Although Scotty really desires a motorcycle, his parents buy him a $2500 classic banjo. Still wanting the cycle, Scotty obtains a loan from banker Gale Gordon using the banjo as collateral. When Scotty shows up with his new motorcycle, his parents ask him to perform a solo on his new instrument at a political rally where the parents will be singing. But Scotty declines. However, being a really good son, Scotty eventually attends the rally and does a solo on the banjo after trading in his motorcycle.

Ironically, Scotty Plummer, nicknamed "Prince of the Banjo," was killed in a motorbike accident in the Bermuda's in 1992.

Bungle Abbey

In 1970, Desi Arnaz attempted to produce a feature film about a monk who is asked by his Abbott to leave the monastery and go out into the world to determine why the Abbey's cheese is not selling. Titled *The Gentle Martyrdom of Brother Bertram*, the monk contacts a high-powered salesman to help with his investigation. Coincidentally, the salesman is faced with the possibility of being investigated by the U.S. Senate and so decides to flee to the Abbey while Brother Bertram enjoys the pleasure of mundane everyday life. Desi wanted Don Rickles for the film, but it is not clear if Rickles would play Brother Bertram or the high-pressure salesman.

The movie was never made, but ten years later, the ex-Mrs. Arnaz tried her own hand at a broad comedy series about monks in an Abbey. *Bungle Abbey* was the only comedy pilot that Lucille Ball not only produced but also directed by herself although, informally, Lucy would direct episodes of *The Lucy Show* and *Here's Lucy* often overruling the real director's instructions.

Made in 1980, *Bungle Abbey* starred Lucy's nemesis from her prior two sitcoms – Gale Gordon as the abbot heading a motley group of monks. The pilot, for NBC, featured Charlie Callas as Brother Charles whose character specialized in bizarre sound effects and celebrity impersonations that were part of Callas' nightclub act; Guy Marks as Brother Hush, so named because he didn't speak but communicated through pantomime; Graham Jarvis as Brother Virgil, the resident cook not known for flavorful dishes; Gino Conforti as Brother Gino, the bell ringer who, because of his slight build, when pulling the rope to ring the bell would disappear up the belfry, and Peter Palmer as Brother Peter, the young, handsome monk.

Written by Seaman Jacobs and Fred S. Fox, the story line of the pilot was played very broadly with plenty of slapstick moments such as a scene with the monks stomping on grapes to make their wine and ending up with purple legs and feet.

The Abbey has to raise $5000 for the local orphanage. The abbot wants to do this by selling more of the Abbey's fruits and chesses, but Brother Charles recommends selling the portrait of the Abbey's founder, Brother Bungle, to raise the funds. While the abbot is away, Brother Charles invites an art dealer to the Abbey to purchase the painting. To increase the price, Brother Charles poses as an art dealer himself bidding against the real dealer. The portrait sells for $10,000. When the abbot finds that the painting has been sold and discovers that Brother Hush has painted an exact copy, he contacts the art dealer who bought the portrait because the abbot believes the monks sold the buyer the copy and not the original. The abbot has the buyer take both paintings.

NBC decided not to turn *Bungle Abbey* into a series.

Although Lucille Ball Productions was never able to launch a television series not starring its owner, the company did produce, along with Aaron Spelling, one other situation comedy starring Ms. Ball. Created by Madelyn Davis and Bob Carroll, Jr., *Life with Lucy* for ABC could have been titled *The Mother-in-Law and the Father-in Law*. Lucy played Lucy Barker, a widow and grandmother whose daughter Margo (Ann Dusenberry) married Ted McGibbon (Larry Anderson). Ted's father, Curtis McGibbon (Gale Gordon), co-owns M & B Hardware with Lucy allowing the two stars to engage in plenty of slapstick and sight gags. Even at age seventy-five, Lucy was reluctant to change her style of comedy as seen

Madelyn Pugh Martin Davis and Bob Carroll, Jr. who penned various scripts for all four Lucy series – I Love Lucy, The Lucy Show, Here's Lucy, *and* Life with Lucy.

not only in *Life with Lucy* but also in the two pilots her company produced for NBC.

As Tim Brooks and Earle Marsh in their book, *The Complete Directory to Prime-Time Network and Cable TV Shows*, describe this effort:

> Probably the most widely anticipated new series – and most embarrassing flop – of the 1986 season was this ill-conceived comedy that marked the return of Lucille Ball to series television after 12 years. In order to get her, ABC had

to promise a huge salary, complete creative control, no pilot or testing before preview audiences, and a guaranteed time slot on the fall schedule. What it got was an unimaginative rehash of the Lucy shows of many years before, only this time with a 75-year-old star.[71]

But to be fair, Ms. Ball may have decided to stick with the type of comedy that made her a TV icon because, when she deviated from her "Lucy" character, the audience and critics were unkind. For example, in the TV specials she made after *Here's Lucy*, such as "Three for Two" co-starring Jackie Gleason, and "What Now, Catherine Curtis," Lucy played characters far removed from her typical comedic ones. The public just didn't seem to accept the actress in any role other than her "Lucy" persona.

Life with Lucy lasted for only two months airing eight episodes before the network canceled it. Ms. Ball passed away three years later in 1989.

Appendix A: The Comedy Episodes that Might Have Been

While the main focus of this book is on Desilu's unsold pilots and unproduced specials, several of the Desilu comedy series described in Chapter 1 had scripts written for episodes that were never made. This appendix describes many of these unproduced episodes.

I Love Lucy

While, as far as can be determined, this classic situation comedy had no unproduced episodes, producer and head writer Jess Oppenheimer indicated that there was a scene from "Lucy Tells the Truth" where the second act had to be re-written because Desi refused to have his character cheat on his federal income taxes.

In the installment, Ricky bets Lucy $100 that she can't go for twenty-four hours without telling white lies. She is brutally honest with everyone in the first act. The original second act had her receiving a phone call from IRS auditor, Mr. Miller, about meeting with her and her husband the following night to go over their tax return. Even though Ricky doesn't want truth-telling Lucy to be in the meeting, she insists on attending. Ricky is concerned that he didn't retain all his receipts for certain deductions and simply guessed at certain amounts.

The next evening, Mr. Miller visits the Ricardo's apartment and begins asking Ricky about the $1500 in entertainment expenses for which Ricardo can't produce all the receipts. Miller also questions his deduction of $1200 for his wardrobe with Lucy indicating that she thinks the amount is excessive. In addition, Ricky took a deduction for a business trip to Louisville, Kentucky where his band performed at the time of the Kentucky Derby. Lucy blurts out that her husband won at the horse track but no winnings were indicated on the return. Miller leaves saying that he will let the Ricardo's know how much more they owe the federal government.

After he departs, Lucy divulges that the man was not really from the IRS. She wanted to play a trick on Ricky and so asked for a man from the Actors Guild to pose as a tax auditor. The real Mr. Miller will stop by later. The doorbell rings, and the actor that Lucy had hired sight unseen arrives saying that he is late because the Actors Guild had given him the wrong address meaning that the real tax auditor had already been there and received the honest truth about the Ricardo's income tax return.

An entirely new second act was written for the episode in which Lucy's fibs end up landing her a job as a knife-thrower's target.[72]

Willy

Although it lasted for only one season, *Willy*, starring June Havoc, had at least three scripts written which were never filmed. The situations in all the scripts deal with Willy taking cases involving individuals inhabiting dwellings that they do not own.

In "Willy vs the Frisbie Ghost" by Howard Harris, the female attorney takes the case of Mrs. Frisbie who has leased her home to a murder mystery writer, Charles B.B. La Scarza, for a year. However, after staying in the house for a few weeks, the writer leaves claiming it is haunted. Willy doesn't think his story is creditable and so she agrees to his bet to stay one night in the house by herself. If she does, he will not only pay the full year's rent but also kick in a six month's bonus. During the night at the house, Willy hears hollow laughs and clinking chains but what really frightens her is the specter of a pirate near the fireplace. She flees the house losing the bet.

The following day, Willy scans La Sacrza's novels to see if any included a scene with a ghost like the one she witnessed. She discovers such a scene and finds that the writer really wanted to break the lease because he couldn't concentrate on his work in such a quiet place. Willy sues him for $25,000 for mental anguish and informs the writer that she recorded a discussion about him using a tape recorder to play the ghostly sound effects. The sound effects are what Willy heard during the night. However, she cannot account for the specter of the pirate.

In "Willy and Gypsy Jack" by Louis Pelletier, Willy handles the case of a carnival gypsy known as Gypsy Jack Columbus and his three daughters – Nina, Pinta, and Santa Maria. Jack has been arrested for trespassing in an abandoned house. Willy has a private hearing with Judge Cogswell about the case. She contends that Jack can't be charged with trespassing since the house is really his. Because the dwelling has been vacant for a number of years, and Jack was the first person to take possession after the abandonment, he legally owns the place. Nevertheless, the next day, Jack decides to return to the carnival.

The third unproduced script, titled "Willy and the Hobo" by Bill Bast and Ted Hartman, was similar in theme to the proposed "Gypsy Jack" episode. Willy takes a liking to a hobo named Be Boe whom the local sheriff is trying to evict from an old railroad car. Willy advises the hobo not to vacate the car since the sheriff has no jurisdiction in the matter – only the railroad police can tell him to leave the car. The next day she consults her law books and concludes that Be Boe has the right to stay in the railroad car based on the right of possession as long as the railroad doesn't instruct him to leave. Willy goes to inform Be Boe of this and finds chickens around the boxcar that a nearby farmer has complained to the sheriff are missing. Willy and Be Boe return the hens as the sheriff arrives to investigate. The two have to hide in 200 pound feed bags to avoid being seen and then get locked in the chicken coop and have to struggle out of a small window in the coop to avoid being caught by the farmer.

The Ann Sothern Show

TV writer Ruth Brooks Flippen developed a treatment for a never-produced episode of *The Ann Sothern Show* called "Service with a Smile." Katy O'Connor and her friend and workmate Olive observe the Award Dinner of the Good Fellowship Society being given in the Crystal Room of the Bartley House. The recipient of the Good Fellowship Plaque is accountant Ray Pepperidge who, in his thank-you speech, calls his wife by his pet name for her – Snuffy. This revelation mortifies his wife, and they have a big fight bringing up twenty-five years of petty grievances and annoyances.

Pepperidge moves out of his home and takes a room at the Bartley House where everyone treats him like the king of the hotel. He loves the service so much that he doesn't want to return home. To entice him to go back to his wife, Katy quickly dictates a memo to Olive for the entire hotel staff requesting that they provide Pepperidge with lousy service. The orders were to apply only to Mr. Pepperidge, but Olive becomes confused and makes out the memo to apply to all of the hotel's guests causing an uproar in the hotel. Katy is able to get the establishment back in order but, in the meantime, Pepperidge decides to go back home and reconcile with his wife.

The Lucy Show

Based on the Jack Donohue Collection at the American Heritage Center, it appears that at least four scripts for *The Lucy Show* were never produced.

"Lucy and Vivian Fight over Harry" was written in September 1962 by Madelyn Davis, Bob Carroll Jr., Bob Schiller, and Bob Weiskopf about Lucy and Viv's attempts at dating.

Viv decides to dump her boyfriend Eddie Collins (Donald Briggs) thinking he is taking her for granted. At the same time, Lucy decides to end her relationship with neighbor Harry Connors (Dick Martin) believing like Viv that Harry is taking her for granted. When Lucy tells Harry that she doesn't want to go to a Broadway musical with him, he asks Viv who gladly accepts the invitation.

While Lucy is waiting for Viv to come to breakfast the morning after her date with Harry, Jerry and Sherman bring home an old, tattered football dummy they found. When Viv enters through the front door, Lucy learns that she was not asleep at all but is just returning from her date. Lucy begins to become jealous of Viv and Harry. Chris, Lucy's daughter, suggests that her mother fight fire with fire and let Harry see her with her own date. Since Lucy can't find a date at the last minute, she decides to pretend that the football dummy which she names "Charlie" is her date. Using a helium balloon for its head with a Halloween mask over the balloon, she proceeds in setting up the dummy at a table so he can be viewed in silhouette through a window with the blinds drawn.

While at Harry's, Viv begins criticizing his cooking, and Harry confesses that he still likes Lucy. Viv decides to take Eddie back. Lucy stops by Harry's place to inform him and Viv that she has a date for the night. After Lucy leaves, Viv and Harry convince themselves that Lucy is telling a fib about a date. But then, the two see Lucy and "Charlie" through the window with Lucy serving him champagne and pretending to have a conversation with him. Lucy slaps Charlie on the back making the dummy pitch forward with Viv and Harry concluding that he is drunk. Lucy then begins dancing with Charlie causing the helium filled balloon to levitate above the dummy's body with Lucy having to affix it to the body again.

As the script describes, "Lucy and Charlie continue dancing and if possible, they do the twist. We haven't any idea how Lucy can get the dummy to look like he's doing the twist, but it's worth a try to see Lucy twisting in silhouette,"[73]

After the dance scene, Harry sees the dummy appear to embrace Lucy causing Harry's jealousy to increase. He decides to go next door. When Lucy hears someone at her door, Lucy hides the dummy in the closet and opens the front door to find Eddie Collins wanting to see Viv. Eddie sits where the dummy was as Harry strides through the door and, assuming Eddie is the man Lucy was with, Harry hits him on the nose. To calm the situation, Lucy reveals the dummy. She gives the dummy a kiss making his balloon head pop and shrivel up. Harry says, "Hey, you never kissed me like that!".[74]

This episode was canceled before filming apparently because of difficulty in trying to film the scene with Lucy and the football dummy in silhouette. Also, the character of Harry Connors was due to be written out of the series, and Lucy and Desi didn't want to film an episode that Lucy was really in love with Harry.

Dated October 6, 1963 and written by Davis, Carroll, Jr., Schiller and Weiskopf, "Lucy Plays Basketball" involved a physically complicated final act that may have led to it never being made. Lucy and Viv are members of an all-female basketball team, "Mooney's Mustangs," sponsored by Theodore Mooney's bank. Mooney threatens to withdraw sponsorship because the team has yet to win a game. Lucy pleads with the banker to allow the team one more chance to win a game against the best team in the league, "Webster's Wildcats." Mooney agrees with Lucy planning extra practice sessions and having the members cut out fattening foods and going to bed early.

Viv has problems obeying the training rules, but Lucy insists. Late at night, Lucy sneaks into the kitchen for an ice cream cone. When Viv awakens to investigate the noise, Lucy quickly hides the cone under her pajama top. When she sits up, pieces of the cone drop on the floor. Viv suspends Lucy from the team, but, after Lucy asks for another chance, Viv makes her the locker room attendant with the possibility, if she does well in that position, that she may allow her to play again.

Later, at practice, Lucy attempts to deliver six or seven basketballs to the team but keeps being interrupted thus having to drop all the balls and pick them up again. She also has to inflate one of the balls using a hand pump not noticing that the ball is becoming bigger and bigger until it explodes.

Trying to save money for the team, Lucy sends their uniforms to a laundry instead of the dry cleaners causing them to shrink to baby doll size. Lucy searches for new uniforms, but all she can find are those from the 1915 era consisting of dark bloomers, black stockings, and navy blue middy blouses. The team doesn't want to wear them, but Mooney, not wanting to forfeit the game to Webster's Wildcats, demands that they put them on.

The game begins with Lucy back on the team. She distracts the opponent by yelling that Rock Hudson is in the stands causing her opponent to lose concentration with Lucy scoring and then scoring again. She continues to score by making almost impossible plays such as one standing on the back of a teammate who bent down to find her contact lens. Near the end of the game, Lucy has the ball but dribbles it in the wrong direction. Viv has to run after her and grabs her by her bloomers which rip. All of her teammates form a circle around her to hide the torn bloomers. The team gets a timeout so that a woman from the bleachers can quickly repair the tear. However, in the rush to fix the tear, Viv and Lucy end up sown together.

When play resumes, Lucy and Viv along with a member from the other team, jump together. Lucy, getting the jump, tips the ball behind her over Viv's head. Viv, facing the direction in which the ball went, chases it with Lucy back pedaling as fast as she can. Viv gets the ball and starts dribbling toward the basket with Lucy running backwards right behind her. Lucy wants Viv to pass her the ball but Viv, facing the basket, wants to shoot. She raises the ball above her head. As she does, Lucy reaches up and back and steals the ball from Viv. Lucy looks up and backwards toward the basket and tosses the ball backwards over her head through the basket with her team winning the game. As both Viv and Lucy bend over to hug their sons who are congratulating them, another loud ripping noise is heard as Lucy and Viv are parted. They start backing off the basketball court with their hands behind them to cover their torn bloomers.

Bob Carroll Jr. and Madelyn Davis along with Bill O'Hallaren wrote two *Lucy Show* scripts - "Lucy Flies a Helicopter" dated August 16, 1963 and "Lucy Is a Girl Friday" dated November 26, 1963. Both scripts begin the same way with Lucy and Viv watching handsome commentator Brett Hampton on his television program where he describes his world travels and, in the helicopter script, does traffic updates for the evening news. On air, Hampton announces that he needs a new Girl Friday to replace the current occupant of that position who is getting married. Both Lucy and Viv want to apply for the job. After arguing about who should get the job, they both agree that neither should apply to keep peace between them. However, Lucy being Lucy secretly decides to go to the TV station to vie for the position. Whom should she see there but Viv along with several other applicants?

When Lucy breaks her pencil while filling out the employment application, she looks in her purse for another writing instrument and finds a toy mouse that she had confiscated from her son and Viv's son after being scared by it. She decides to wind it up and let it loose in the room causing the other women, including Viv, to hastily beat a retreat leaving only her as the sole remaining applicant. Hampton hires her on the spot despite the fact that Lucy has no on-air television experience.

That afternoon Lucy begins her new job doing commercials for the live broadcast. For her first commercial about a hair spray product, Lucy mistakenly applies the product of another sponsor – a spray-on varnish, to her hair. She tries to comb her hair with the comb clicking against her hair with a metallic sound. She reaches up to take hold of a piece of hair only to have the piece snap off. More of her hair snaps off as she begins crying, and the program displays a slide stating "interrupted by technical difficulties." Hampton fires Lucy, but she yearns for a second chance.

In "Lucy Flies a Helicopter," Viv is subsequently hired as Lucy's replacement and goes up in the helicopter with Hampton to assist in traffic reporting. Much to Viv and Brett's surprise, Lucy has stowed away underneath the back seat of the chopper. She emerges saying that she thought Hampton would be alone in the helicopter and that if she did a good job helping him with traffic reports, he would hire her back.

Hampton is then alerted that the Tahitian Queen, a ship that had rescued him during World War II, has run aground. He flies the chopper to the scene hoping to file a human interest story. He requests that they all put on parachutes since they will be over water. In the process, Lucy inadvertently pulls too hard on the ripcord of Viv's chute resulting in the chute opening and billowing out and filling the cockpit.

Once the chute is contained, Hampton, nearing the scene of the Tahitian Queen, gives Lucy a short course on how to fly the copter so he can take some pictures of the ship. Taking over the controls, Lucy causes the helicopter to pitch sharply to one side with Brett falling out the door and disappearing. With his parachute deployed, he goes right into the water near the ship and is rescued.

Lucy tries to find her way back to the nearby airport but becomes lost in the fog. Viv and she end up flying to New York City spotting the Statue of Liberty and landing on top of the United Nations building.

In the script "Lucy Is a Girl Friday," there is no mention of Brett Hampton doing traffic reports from a helicopter. Instead, after Lucy is fired from her Gal Friday position, she tries another way of getting back into Hampton's good graces.

The hair spray sponsor, whom she embarrassed on air, likes a Scottish drum and bagpipe group called the Edinburgh Pipers who, because of a scheduling conflict, had to cancel their appearance on the following day's presentation of the Brett Hampton show. Lucy and Viv visit a Pipers rehearsal to try to convince them to appear on Hampton's program but to no avail. Lucy comes up with a scheme for two pipers, Viv and her, to appear with both dressed in Scottish garb. Viv plays the bagpipes and Lucy the drum. The full Edinburgh Pipers decide, at the last minute, to entertain on the show and, in the end, join Lucy and Viv in a loud performance.

Despite the reworking of the helicopter script into "Lucy Is a Girl Friday," evidently Ms. Ball decided against filming either version.

Endnotes

1. Gene Handsaker, "Hollywood," *Standard-Sentinel*, October 19, 1951.
2. "One-Man Rule," *Variety*, May 18, 1960.
3. Bob Thomas, "Desi Arnaz back at Desilu Studio," *Lake Charles American-Press*, May 7, 1966.
4. Val Adams, "Miss Ball Views Desilu from Top," *The New York Times*, November 20, 1962.
5. Herbert F. Solow and Robert H. Justman, *Inside Star Trek: The Real Story*, New York: Pocket Books, 1996, 5.
6. "Ball, Arnaz Organize Show Company," *The Los Angeles Times*, April 24, 1950.
7. "Chicago, Chicago," *The Billboard*, June 10, 1950.
8. Wayne Oliver, "June Havoc, Prettiest Legal Eagle, Has a Couple of Problems on TV," *Press and Sun Bulletin*, February 13, 1955.
9. Dave Kaufman, "On All Channels," *Variety*, May 9, 1958.
10. Lloyd Shearer, "Desi – His Life without Lucy," *Albuquerque Journal*, October 7, 1962.
11. Coyne Steven Sanders and Tom Gilbert, *Desilu: The Story of Lucille Ball and Desi Arnaz*, New York: William Morrow and Company, Inc., 1993, 273.
12. "Colgate Theatre," Telepix Reviews, *Variety*, August 21, 1958.
13. Coyne Steven Sanders and Tom Gilbert, *Desilu*, 153.
14. Rob Edelman and Audrey Kuperberg, *Meet the Mertzes: The Life Stories of I Love Lucy's Other Couple*, Los Angeles: Renaissance Books: 1999, 159.
15. Frank Castelluccio and Alvin Walker, *The Other Side of Ethel Mertz: The Life Story of Vivian Vance*, Manchester, Connecticut: Knowledge, Ideas & Trends Inc., 1998, 231.
16. Jim Brosnan, *The Long Season: The Classic Inside Account of a Baseball Year, 1959*, New York: HarperCollins, 1960, 7-8.
17. Dave Kaufman, "On All Channels," *Variety*, May 20, 1955.
18. Desi Arnaz, *A Book*, New York: William Morrow and Company, Inc., 1976, 275.
19. Joseph Finnigan, "Sinatra, Desi Part Company," *The Pittsburgh Press*, April 7, 1961.
20. "Plan to Start Re-Run 'Lucy' Telecasts in '56," *Variety*, March 11, 1954.
21. "Tele Follow-Up Comment," *Variety*, September 10, 1958.
22. "Lloyd Nolan Rebels When Father Duffy Is Chased from 'Kitchen,' Romance Added," *Variety*, March 30, 1956.
23. Dave Kaufman, "On All Channels," *Variety*, November 6, 1956.
24. Desi Arnaz, *A Book*, 305.
25. Quoted in Peter Prescott Tonguette, *Orson Welles Remembered: Interviews with His Actors, Editors, Cinematographers and Magicians*, Jefferson, North Carolina: McFarland and Company, Inc., 2007, 33.
26. Coyne Steven Sanders and Tom Gilbert, *Desilu*, 121.

27 Ibid.
28 "Welles, Arnaz Join to Film 'Theater' Series," *The Billboard*, April 14, 1956.
29 Quinn Martin, "The Woman in the Case," David Harmon Papers, Wisconsin Historical Society.
30 William Spier, Letter to Sam Jaffe, William Spier and June Havoc Collection, Wisconsin Historical Society, undated.
31 Adrian Spies, "The Arlene Dahl Show," Adrian Spies Collection, Wisconsin Historical Society, undated.
32 Desi Arnaz, *A Book*, 295.
33 Ibid., 297.
34 "Desilu in $7,500,000 TV Splurge," *Variety*, February 20, 1958.
35 "Westinghouse Desilu Playhouse," Television Reviews, *Variety*, February 22, 1960.
36 "Midgets & Missiles," *Variety*, May 13, 1959.
37 "Desilu Playhouse," Tele Follow-Up Comment, *Variety*, May 13, 1959.
38 Hal Humphrey, "All Those TV Buckskin Heroes Did Wrong by Jane Russell," *Detroit Free Press*, January 25, 1959.
39 "$1 Mil Outlay for 1963-64 Pilots Record for Desilu," *Variety*, October 25, 1962.
40 "This Is Alice," Telepix Reviews, *Variety*, October 9, 1958.
41 "Audition Game Show as 'Lucy' Replacement," *Variety*, January 26, 1966.
42 Bob Thomas, "Story of Gambling Queen to Be Filmed," *Alton Evening Telegraph*, December 19, 1949.
43 Gladys Hurlbut, *Next Week, East Lynne*, New York: E.P. Dutton & Company, Inc., 1950, 16.
44 Ibid., 160.
45 George S, Kaufman and Leueen Mac Grath, *Fancy Meeting You Again*, Dramatists Play Service, Inc., 1951, 31.
46 Richardson Wright, *Forgotten Ladies*, Philadelphia: J.B. Lippincott Company, 1928, 167.
47 Michael Ellis, undated memo to Lucy Kroll, Lucy Kroll Papers, Manuscript Division, Library of Congress.
48 Dorothy Hechtlinger, letter to Lucy Kroll, September 28, 1959, Lucy Kroll Papers, Manuscript Division, Library of Congress.
49 Edgar Penton, "'Glynis' Seen as Combination of 'Lucy' and the 'Thin Man,'" *Green Bay Press-Gazette*, September 29, 1963.
50 "Glynis," Telepix Reviews, *Variety*, September 27, 1963.
51 Quoted in Caryl Flinn, *Brass Diva: The Life and Legends of Ethel Merman*, Berkeley, CA: University of California Press, 2007, 341-342.
52 Alex Freeman, "TV Closeup," *Star-Gazette*, August 11, 1963.

53 "Desilu Shelves Pair," *Variety*, February 20, 1963.

54 Dwayne Hickman and Joan Roberts Hickman, *Forever Dobie: The Many Lives of Dwayne Hickman*, New York: Carol Publishing Group, 1994, 163.

55 Jack Donohue and Will Grefe, *Letters of a Hoofer to His Ma*, New York: Cosmopolitan Book Corporation, 1931, 142-43.

56 Earl Wilson, "On Broadway," *The Des Moines Register*, February 28, 1966.

57 Hal Humphrey, "Comedy Writing Funny as a Crutch," *The Los Angeles Times*, December 23, 1965.

58 Walt Hackett, "Frank Merriwell, Hero, Will Be Revived on TV," *Lansing State Journal*, April 22, 1951.

59 Dave Kaufman, "On All Channels," *Variety*, May 26, 1964.

60 Sam Rolfe, "Prospectus for *The Long Hunt of April Savage*," Sam Rolfe Collection, American Heritage Center, undated, 1.

61 Gene Roddenberry, First Draft Treatment, March 11, 1964.

62 Herbert F. Solow, *Inside Star Trek*, 59-60.

63 Dave Ebersole, "Assignment: Earth," Orion Press, retrieved July 9, 2019.

64 David Alexander, *Star Trek Creator: The Authorized Biography of Gene Roddenberry*, New York: Penguin Books, 1994, 332.

65 Desi Arnaz, *A Book*, 295.

66 Desi Arnaz, "Sweeping Bird Cages Easier Than Making a TV Sweep,' *Variety*, October 31, 1967.

67 Dean Gysel, "Carol Channing Show Looks Good, on Paper," *Kingsport Times*, March 14, 1967.

68 Ben Falke, "Desi Arnaz Tells How He Invented the TV Rerun," *Daily News*, June 23, 1974.

69 Marilyn Beck, "Film's Co-stars Finally on Same Coast," *The Courier-News*, October 15, 1970.

70 Peter J. Boyle, "Lucille Ball Stars in 'Lucy Moves to NBC' Airing Tonight," *Hattiesburg American*, February 8, 1980.

71 Tim Brooks and Earle Marsh, *The Complete Directory to Prime Time Network and Cable TV Shows: 1946 – Present*, Ninth Edition, New York: Ballantine Books, 2007, 792.

72 Jess Oppenheimer with Gregg Oppenheimer, Appendix B, "The Unperformed *I Love Lucy*," *Laughs, Luck . . . and Lucy*, Syracuse, New York: Syracuse University Press, 1996, 249-257.

73 Bob Carroll, Jr., Madelyn Davis, Bob Weiskopf, Bob Schiller, *The Lucy Show*, "Lucy and Vivian Fight over Harry," Jack Donohue Collection, American Heritage Center, September 17, 1962, 37.

74 Ibid., 42.

Index

A
Abbott Mysteries: 39
Adventures of Jack London: 44
Adventures of a Model: 12
Aldo Ray Project: 21
Alfred of the Amazon: 141-142
All about Barbara: 14-15
Always April: 16-17
Anatomy of: 64
Ann Sothern Show: 8-9, 16-18, 178-179
Anso: 8, 16
Anthology of Suspense: 55-56
A-Okay O'Shea: 123-124
The Arlene Dahl Show: 62-63
Arnaz, Desi
  as actor: 3, 6, 12, 58, 67-70, 72, 97, 98, 99, 103, 116, 164, 165, 176
  as director: 65, 160
  as producer: xi- xiii, 1, 2, 4-6, 8-9, 12-15, 18-21, 24-29, 33- 37, 46, 49, 54, 57-59, 61, 62, 65, 67, 68, 74, 76-77, 84, 89-90, 97, 111, 117, 121, 123, 136, 156, 158, 160-163, 172, 180
  as writer: 76, 173
Arnaz, Jr., Desi: 116, 160, 166
Arnaz, Lucie: 116, 166, 171
Assignment: Earth: 153-154

B
Ball, Lucille
  as actress: xi, 1-5, 7, 9-10, 12-14, 21-22, 24-25, 43, 46, 56, 58, 65, 67-68, 70, 72-73, 97-116, 125-126, 161, 166-167, 170-171, 173, 175-177, 179-183
  as director: 172
  as producer: xii- xiii, 96-97, 119, 122, 129, 134-136, 143, 166, 171-175
Bandwagon: 76-77
The Big Circuit: 44-45
The Black Arrow: 37
Blazing Beulah from Butte: 97
Blees, Robert: 124, 137, 143, 144, 148
Blood, Of the A.E.F.: 149
Bob Hope Show: 20
Borderline: 144
Briskin, Mort: 37, 40, 44, 50, 51, 54, 63, 74, 87, 88, 117, 163
Bromfield, John: 51, 52
Bungle Abbey: 172-173
Byington, Spring: 6, 68

C
Caballero: 41-42
Calhoun, Rory: 7, 41, 47, 68, 163
The Carol Channing Show: 160-161
Carroll, Jr., Bob: 2, 3, 4, 7, 10, 14, 15, 65, 70, 100, 111, 112, 116, 159, 160, 161, 162, 171, 173, 179, 180, 181
Chairman of the Board: 163-164
Chick Bowdrie, Texas Ranger: 41
C.I.C. (Counter-Intelligence Corps): 84-87
Cleat Adams: 144
Cloud Nine: 28
Code 100: 148-149
College Humor: 22
The Con Man: 91-92
Corky/Love Me, Love Queenie: 139
Country Doctor: 35-36
Cowboy Detective: 49

D
Dallas: 51-52
Davis, Madelyn Pugh Martin: 2, 3, 4, 7, 10, 14, 15, 65, 70, 100, 111-112, 116, 159, 160, 161, 162, 171, 173, 179, 180, 181
December Bride: 6-7
Desi Arnaz Productions: xiii, 63, 158
Desi Arnaz Unproduced Specials: 9, 117-118, 158

Desilu: xi, xii, xiii, 1, 4-12, 15-16, 18-25, 27-29, 31-32, 34-39, 41-42, 44-47, 49, 51-56, 59- 60, 62-65, 67-68, 70, 74-78, 80, 83-84, 88, 90-91, 93-97, 100, 102, 107, 109-111, 116-117, 119-120, 122- 24, 126-27, 129, 131, 134-37, 139, 143-44, 146-48, 153-54, 156, 158, 161, 166, 176
Desilu's Little People: 94
Donegan's Six Guns: 78
Donohue, Jack: 129-130, 179
Downbeat: 34-35
Dr. Augustus Van Dusen Mysteries: 80-82
Dr. Domingo: 164-165
Duncan Maclain Mysteries: 83

E
Eddie Guillan Project: 19
EM + C2, Inc.: 140
Ernestine: 13-14
Escapade: 144
Exclusively Connie: 124

F
Fair Exchange: 24, 28, 132
Famous Artists Anthologies: 61-62
The Farmer from Palermo: 132-133
Fast Freight: 35
Father Duffy of Hell's Kitchen: 47-49
Floyd Gibbons, Reporter: 90-91
The Flying Fish: 49
For Men Only: 63
Frank Merriwell: 139
Frawley, William: 3, 25-26, 67-68, 72, 112, 114

G
Glynis: 18, 119
Goldman, Hal: 119, 126, 133, 138
The Good Old Days: 138-139
Gordon, Gale: 3, 10, 13, 20, 65, 166, 172-173
Grand Jury: 51

Greatest Show on Earth: 45
The Greenhorns: 143-144
The Guardians: 44
Guestward Ho!: 24, 27-28, 132
Gussie, My Girl: 15, 161-162

H
Ham and Davey: 162-163
Harrigan and Son: 24, 29, 132
Havoc, June: 4-5, 59, 65, 177
Here's Lucy: 2, 10, 22, 101, 129, 166-167, 170-172, 175
Hey, Teacher: 129
High Noon: 147
His Highness and O'Hara: 134
The Holidays Abroad: 31-32
Homicide Squad: 42
The Hoofer: 129-131
Hooray for Hollywood: 137
Hope, Bob: xi, 10, 20, 111-115
Howard, Cy: 21, 28, 32, 122, 127, 131, 135

I-J
I Love Lucy: xi, xii, xiii, 1-8, 10-12, 14-15, 19, 24-27, 34-35, 43, 56, 67, 97, 99, 111-112, 116, 119, 159, 161, 176-177
I Married a Martian: 136
Intelligence Squad: 50-51
John Wesley Hardin Family Project: 49-50
Jon Whiteley/Vincent Winter Project: 93-94
Johnny Cinderella: 78-79
Jurow, Martin: 119, 123, 127, 144
Just Off Broadway: 11

K
Katz, Oscar: xiii, 119, 124, 129, 143-144, 148
Klein, Larry: 119, 126, 133, 138
Kraft Mystery Theatre: 80, 83

L

The Lady Is a Champ: 124-125
Land's End: 163
The Last Marshall: 38
Leeds, Martin: xii, 34-35, 38, 49, 52, 58, 157
Life with Lucy: 173-175
Locust 4-3931: 45
The Long Hunt of April Savage: 144-146
Lucie Arnaz Show: 170-171
Lucille Ball-Desi Arnaz Show (aka *Lucy-Desi Comedy Hour*): 1, 67-68, 73, 99, 109
Lucille Ball Productions: xiii, 166, 173
Lucille Ball Specials
 produced: 116, 170, 171, 175
 unproduced: 100-116, 166-170
The Lucy Show: xi, xii, 2, 9-10, 13, 20, 22, 65, 96, 116, 120, 129, 167, 172, 179-183

M

Maggie Brown: 121-122, 123
The Man from Telegraph Hill: 53-54
The Man Nobody Knows: 156
Man of Letters: 28-29
Mannix: 39, 119, 143
Martin, Dick: 21, 22, 179
Martin, Quinn: 14, 15, 52, 60
The Mertzes: 25-27
Mickey and the Contessa: 32
Mission: Impossible: xi, xiii, 119, 142, 143, 144, 155-157
Mr. Tutt: 36
Mother Is the Law: 126-127
The Mothers-in-Law: 158, 159, 163
Murphy, George: 25, 62, 68, 117
The Music Mart: 171-172
My Favorite Husband: 2-4
My Lucky Penny: 127-128
My Son, The Doctor: 133-134
My Uncle Louie: 131-132
My Wife's Brother: 21-22

N

National Telefilm Associates (NTA): 36, 37, 39, 51, 52, 93
Nightclub: 77
The Night Hunters: 146
Night Watchman: 20
No Man Walks Alone: 54

O

O.C.D. (Official Crime Division): 54
Official Detective: 55
Oh, Nurse: 18
Oppenheimer, Jess: 2-4, 10, 119, 125, 131, 176
The Orson Welles Show: 56-58

P-Q

Pandora: 17-18
Papa G.I.: 131
The Pearls: 127
Penelope's Boys: 141
Personal Report, Inc.: 38-39
Phil Harris/Alice Faye Show: 29-30
Police Story: 149-150
Private Eyeful: 39-40
Privateer: 50

R

The Recruiters: 134
Relatively Yours: 95-96
Rikki of the Islands: 94
Ritz Brothers: 19
Roddenberry, Gene: 119, 146-151, 153-154
The Rolling Stones: 24
Rookie Cop: 37
Rowan, Dan: 21, 22

S

Sad Sack: 20
Schiller, Bob: 4, 8, 10, 24, 27-28, 30-31, 139, 179-180
Secret Service Agent: 52
Security Agent: 40-41
The Seekers: 89-90

Sheriff of Cochise: 52
Sheriff Squad: 42-44
Sinatra, Frank: xi, 34
Sothern, Ann: 8-9, 17-18, 68, 109, 158
Spanner: 33
Spellbound: 143
Spier, William: 4, 35, 47, 55, 59, 61, 65-66, 84, 86
Spies, Adrian: 45-46, 62, 68, 77
The Star: 98-99
Star Trek
  pilot: 150-151
  series: xi, xiii, 45, 119, 143, 144, 147, 153, 154
Swingin' Together: 22-23

T
Tales of Allan Pinkerton: 47
Ten Top Wanted Men: 52
That Townsend Girl: 99
The Texan: 41, 47, 49, 100
This Is Alice: 93
Those Whiting Girls: 7-8
Three in a Row: 28
The Two of Us: 32
Tonight in Havana: 39
Trio: 156-157
21 Beacon Street: 157

U-V
U.S. Air Force: 74-76
The United States Immigration Story: 65-66
U.S. Marshal: 52
The Unteachables: 135-136
The Untouchables: xi, xii, 9, 34, 42, 45-47, 72-75, 84, 88-91, 135
Vacation with Pay: 137-138
Vance, Vivian: 3, 9-10, 25-27, 67-68, 72, 102, 112-113
Venus Mahoney: 98
Victor Borge Comedy Theatre: 64-65
Villa Marina: 63
The Violaters: 44

W-X
Walter Winchell Files: 46-47
Weiskopf, Bob: 4, 8, 10, 24, 27-28, 30-31, 139, 179-180
Westinghouse-Desilu Playhouse (aka *Desilu Playhouse*): 21, 45, 55, 67-68, 70, 72-75, 77-80, 98-100, 117
Where There's Smokey: 20-21
The Whirlwind: 148
Whirlybirds: 42-43
The White Knights: 87-89
Whiting, Barbara and Margaret: 7
Wildcat: 111-116
The Wildcatters: 37
Willy: 4-5, 177-178
Winchell, Walter: 46-47
Woman in the Case: 59-61
Working Girls: 123

Y-Z
Yankee Gunfighter: 154
You Can't Win Them All: 30-31
You Don't Say: 94, 95
Young Man with a Badge: 42
You're Only Young Twice: 24-25
Zoom: 95

www.ingramcontent.com/pod-product-compliance
Lightning Source LLC
Chambersburg PA
CBHW051925160426
43198CB00012B/2039